Team Teaching in Early Childhood

Team Teaching in Early Childhood

Leadership Tools
for Reflective Practice

Uniit Carruyo

Redleaf Press®
www.redleafpress.org
800-423-8309

Published by Redleaf Press
10 Yorkton Court
St. Paul, MN 55117
www.redleafpress.org

First edition 2017
Cover and interior design by Ryan Scheife, Mayfly Design
Cover artwork: "Teamwork symbol. Multicolored hands" © art4all/Shutterstock;
     "Textured background" © marinatakano/Shutterstock.
Typeset in the Chaparral Pro and Whitney typefaces
Printed in the United States of America
24 23 22 21 20 19 18 17   1 2 3 4 5 6 7 8

Library of Congress Cataloging-in-Publication Data
Names: Carruyo, Uniit, author.
Title: Team teaching in early childhood : leadership tools for reflective practice / Uniit Carruyo.
Description: First edition. | St. Paul, MN : Redleaf Press, [2017] |
Includes bibliographical references and index.
Identifiers: LCCN 2016032112 (print) | LCCN 2016054522 (ebook) | ISBN 9781605544885
(pbk.) | ISBN 9781605544892 (ebook)
Subjects: LCSH: Teaching teams—United States | Early childhood education—United States.
Classification: LCC LB1029.T4 C37 2017 (print) | LCC LB1029.T4 (ebook) |
DDC 372.21—dc23
LC record available at https://lccn.loc.gov/2016032112

Printed on acid-free paper

This book is dedicated to Kristin Campagnolo,
who taught me that to teach, you must first love.

*Every experience should do something to prepare a person
for later experiences of a deeper and more expansive
quality. That is the very meaning of growth, continuity,
reconstruction of experience.*

—JOHN DEWEY, *EXPERIENCE AND EDUCATION*

Contents

Foreword

It is not surprising to me that this impressive and appealing book was created by Uniit Carruyo. When she was a student in the Leadership in the Arts program, a unique collaborative program between the Leadership department at the Bank Street College of Education and Parsons School of Design, she took an art course where her assignment was to make a short movie about her journey to class. She filmed the journey of her feet as she made her way through New York City to get to Parsons. This was an example of Uniit's perspective on the world. She attended to the feet, often forgotten by most of us. She pointed out their hard work and used her artistic perspective to make the viewer pay attention and to consider their worth and the possibilities.

In this book she helps us to see the enormous importance of the work done by early childhood educators who are passionate, but not often well-compensated, for their work. She points out the multiple challenges faced by professionals in the field. She brings her expertise as an experienced early childhood educator, leader, and artist to this important work. She finds possibilities and opportunities for professional growth within the day to day functioning of early childhood settings. The needs of the children and their families are at the center of her work.

This book has a firm foundation in theories about leadership and child development. The focus is on the functioning of teams in early childhood settings. In the introduction, the author states that the reason that early childhood educators work in teams is primarily logistical. This is not unique to early childhood settings. Schools at all levels are expected to meet the needs of an increasingly diverse population and individuals working in teams are expected to address the complex needs of the students. Teams bring people together. There is considerable consensus that teams can have significant positive impact on classroom practice and student achievement (Sather 2009, 7; Supovitz and Christman 2003, 8).

The challenge in this work is to get a diverse group of individuals who work together to function as a cohesive team where everyone's contributions are heard, appreciated, and used to solve challenges in educational settings. This challenge is compounded by the fact that in early childhood settings, there tend to be few opportunities for staff members to get together to grow into a team. What can leaders in educational settings do to begin the work to create teams to support the practice of the adults that will lead to strong outcomes for children and their families? This is the question that led the author to inquire about how teams in schools can be more harmonious, satisfying, and productive, and it ultimately led to this book. Here, the reader benefits from the author's journey.

The work of the team begins with self-reflection by the participants. The guiding questions and templates that are used throughout the book support this work of self-examination, and this focus on the self brings clarity to the work of the team. The reflection questions are accessible but tap into deep beliefs about roles, personal strengths, and practices. The answers have the potential to lead to greater self-awareness and compassion for the self and others. These questions and prompts are useful for all educators at all stages of their careers.

Interwoven among the tools, reflections, and prompts are examples of the author's practice and descriptions of the types of interactions that are common to all educators. The author explains and highlights pertinent parts of the theories that support her work and then translates them into practical tools and strategies that facilitate reflection. There are tools for all the stakeholders in school communities: administrators, lead teachers, assistant teachers, and families. Certain tools are for lead teachers who are expected to lead the teams. Other tools are for assistant teachers and some of the tools are for both lead teachers and assistants. The tools are designed for multiple uses and reflect the complexities of this work. The book overall allows for multiple entry points and can be used as either a guide to support with the creation or support of a team. The tools can also be used independently to address a particular need or challenge within a team.

There is a gentleness in this book. It is obvious in the lovely art that surrounds the tools and templates. The gentleness is in the content of the reflective questions. The answers to the questions lead to the identification of strengths and positive attributes. This approach leads to a positive strength-based perspective on colleagues, administrators, children, and their families and makes the work more personally meaningful to all. This book provides an important roadmap for leaders and teachers to ignite the flame that fuels the work that we do. The Buddhist monk Thich Nhat Hanh has stated, "You cannot transmit wisdom or insight to someone else—the seed is already there. A good teacher is someone who touches that seed so it can wake up, sprout, and grow." This book can help teachers and leaders do exactly that.

Ellis E. Scope, PhD
Department of Educational Leadership
Bank Street College of Education

Acknowledgments

I would like to express my gratitude to the people who have made this book possible. I'd like to thank Kara Lomen, Laurie Herrmann, Jim Handrigan, Douglas Schmitz, and everyone at Redleaf Press for their patience with my many questions and for their invaluable insight and guidance in this process.

Thank you to Ellis Scope and Cathleen Wiggins, who taught me what Bank Street leadership looks like and how to lead artfully, and to stand on the shoulders of giants when I feel small. I am grateful for Virginia Varga and Judy Joynt at the Center for Montessori Education (CME), who taught me to look at children with reverence and awe, and for Laura Graham, who has been my trusted colleague for more than twenty years of brainstorming, applauding one another, and imagining possibilities. I thank Gimme! Coffee on State Street in Ithaca, New York, for caffeinating me, always with a friendly smile, as I wrote this book. Thank you to Charles Abelmann and the Barrie School for leadership inspiration and encouragement. Thank you to Heather Frost and Sarah Wharton for their help and expertise in developing signs for use in teaching teams. I'm grateful for every one of my team members over the years, each of whom has taught me something unique and humbling. I wish to offer my heartfelt gratitude to Elizabeth Harrison, Joey Steinhagen, and Aram for offering endless sage advice, calming counsel, and hugs, in that order. And lastly, I'm grateful to my son, Kii, for being the reason my heart has grown big enough to fit in so many other people, too.

Introduction

We in early childhood work in a very particular and intimate way. We serve as an extension of the young child's family. We create a home away from home for our youngest learners. We tend to the emotional, intellectual, and physical needs of these small people, support their parents and caregivers in their roles, and create learning environments where young children can succeed. And we do much of this work in teams of two or more adults cooperating to manage the daily operations of a classroom. This includes supervision, curriculum development, maintaining the classroom environment, and communicating with families.

The reason we work in teams is primarily logistical. State laws mandate certain ratios of adults to children. Children with special rights or specific behavioral plans require one-to-one care. The safety of the children in child care centers and school settings is of utmost importance, and it takes more than one adult to ensure safety and best practices. Many and varied factors contribute to creating a healthy, functioning team. This book seeks to address the need for more intentional conversation about what those factors are—thoughtful leadership with clearly defined goals and roles, compassionate communication, and regular feedback, to name a few.

How many early childhood educators have found themselves in the role of lead or head teacher with no training on supervision, leadership, or adult development? Teacher trainings focus primarily on children's learning, child development, and curriculum design. Offering teachers training on how to lead a team, supervise and orient new teachers in the classroom, and support adult learning is often overlooked.

How many early childhood educators have accepted a position as an assistant teacher and been placed in a team with little or no training on collaboration, orientation to the program, or clarity about their role or the roles of other team members? How much more effective could teams be with a little investment of time to support and integrate assistant teachers into the team?

There are few other professions in which small teams of adults and groups of children spend every day together in one (often small) room. Early childhood education is an inherently intimate, familylike experience. Consider the nature of the work we're doing: teaching Humanity 101. When we teach young children, we are really giving foundational courses to group after group of future adults, teaching them empathy, compassion, kindness, patience, self-confidence, self-reliance, resilience, independence, clear and honest communication, and self-reflection. Most of all, we are teaching them to learn for the sheer joy of learning. The work we do as early childhood educators requires us to be deeply aware of our personal strengths and weaknesses and to be willing to reflect on and refine our teaching practice from day to day and from year to year. All this work is required alongside other adults with whom we may not have much in common outside the classroom.

Often a love of children is what draws people to work in early childhood education, not their experience or educational background. This creates a sort of hierarchy—spoken or unspoken—in which one person has had specialized training in teaching a certain age group, in a certain philosophy, or in a particular educational method, and several other classroom teachers have varying degrees of education or experience. For example, in the Montessori school where I work, only one head teacher is required to have a Montessori teaching certification, and the rest of the team might come from any other discipline. In child care centers, there may be one lead teacher with assistant teachers. In public schools, there may be one lead teacher and paraprofessionals with varying degrees of experience and education.

Due to varying teacher education requirements, lack of formal leadership training for teachers, and scarce professional development opportunities that depend on external resources such as time and money, functioning as a productive team can be challenging for many early childhood educators. For instance, lead teachers may have had specialized training in the age of the children with whom they work, but they may not have had any training in leading adults. Lead teachers who are perfectly comfortable leading a group of young children can feel quite intimidated by leading a group of their peers. Or other team members may have experience in disciplines that seem unrelated— for example, horticulture or finance—and need creative support to apply their experience effectively to an early childhood setting.

When I was studying educational leadership at Bank Street College of Education, I became very interested in team-teaching dynamics and what makes a good team. When I began researching these topics, I found that team teaching in early childhood settings is an overlooked area of education that warrants some focused attention. I asked myself, Are teachers in certification programs getting leadership training to lead their teams? Are teachers hired to be members of a teaching team given training on how to team-teach? Are teams encouraged to collaborate on a deeply meaningful level, or just to get the job done? What makes a team harmonious? And what impact does all this have on young children's learning?

This book is the result of that inquiry. It is intended to help any member of a team practice self-reflection to improve the experience of working in a team. This book is meant for the lead teacher and also contains useful information for the other team members. Within the pages of this book, you will find strategies for communication and reflection exercises to do alone and with your team to look more deeply at the group's dynamic. Some of the reflections are geared toward leaders of the team, some for assistant teachers, and some for any team member. In doing these reflections together and taking the time to have these conversations with your team, you will uncover the potential for a more satisfying and productive team relationship.

Throughout this book, for simplicity, I will refer to the lead or head teacher as the lead. I will refer to any teacher who is not the head or lead teacher as an assistant teacher. Because it is an accurate reflection of the current majority in early childhood, I will use the pronoun *she* to refer to teachers.

I hope this book will provide an entry point to more conversation in your own setting, be it a Montessori school, a child care center, an independent school, or a public school. I will use my own setting as an example throughout the book, and my goal is to provide you with a malleable framework you can adapt to your unique setting and a foundation on which you can build systems to strengthen your team or the teams in your program. Strong teams ensure that the young children in your care have the best chance for success in their learning environments.

Foundations of Team Teaching

Whether you are just starting your work in a team or you find yourself in a team that does not function well, the time you invest now in understanding the big picture will provide the foundation for ensuring that your team is healthy and harmonious.

Define Your Setting

The first step in outlining what an ideal, healthy team in your particular environment looks like is to look closely at your setting so you can define it. Step back and look at the big picture for your organization. In the day-to-day routines of caring for children and families, it's easy to focus on your own classroom and lose sight of the larger view. Recognizing the big picture will allow you to clarify your team's role in the organization and your role in the team.

The reflective questions included in this section will help you define your setting. They will do so by encouraging you to consider how your program's work affects others, what deeper meaning you attribute to your work, and what your professional goals are.

In my Montessori setting, the mission statement is as follows: "We nurture the spirit of each child through meaningful connections with families and our dedication to the principles of Montessori Education" (Ithaca Montessori School 2016). Our values as an organization are love, peace, respect, integrity, and excellence. Our mission and values provide a clear set of guidelines for professional behavior. The mission and values also provide a foundation on which the staff at the school can build our relationships with children and families, shape curriculum, and represent our work in the community.

We are a nonprofit Montessori school located in Ithaca, a small town in central New York. Because we are close to Cornell University and Ithaca College, many of our families include professors, researchers, and graduate students. Many families are bilingual, and most have two full-time working parents. Our school has children from three months to six years old. These details make up who we are and define our identity as an organization.

Such defining details matter because when early childhood professionals know who their families and children are, they can provide a much higher quality of care and learning for children. Defining context clarifies the priorities of the school community, so that teams can align their professional priorities and work together to deliver a curriculum that is truly relevant to the people it serves. The needs of a rural school community will be different from those of an urban one. The needs of a school where most parents work full-time will be different from those of a school where some parents do not do income-earning work. The needs of a school where families have access to many resources will be different from one where families struggle for resources. Geography, socio-economics, and culture affect whom a school serves and how. Recognizing your context and actively responding to it by shaping your professional goals will strengthen your impact on children's learning. It will support your work in teams by ensuring you are all on the same page about *why* you are prioritizing parent education, a certain curriculum, fund-raising, or whatever you choose to prioritize.

Let's look at other early childhood organizations and investigate their mission statements. We have already examined one small, nonprofit, tuition-driven example. A national, publicly funded example is Head Start. The vision of the National Head Start Association (NHSA) is "to lead—to be the untiring voice that will not be quiet until every vulnerable child is served with the Head Start model of support for the whole child, the family and the community—and to advocate—to work diligently for policy and institutional changes that ensure all vulnerable children and families have what they need to succeed. NHSA's mission is to coalesce, inspire, and support the Head Start field as a leader in early childhood development and education" (NHSA 2016).

Head Start clearly states its mission and values, and with this statement it provides a framework for its employees. The principles of leadership, persistence, advocacy, hard work, and dedication to the organization on behalf of children and families all shine through in this mission statement, and for those employed by Head Start, it is necessary to embody these principles.

Even a few simple, descriptive words can help educators in an organization understand what the organization values. Schools use words such as *dream*, *dare*, *be*, *engage*, and *empower* to boldly describe their goals for children. When teams are aligned by such big-picture values, they can strive to embody these values in the work they do with one another, children, and families. For instance, if teams know their organization values daring, they can feel free to make bold choices in their work. If teams know their organization values democracy above all else, their choices with children and families will reflect that commitment to democracy.

Take some time to reflect on what you most wish for the children in your care. Is the most important outcome for these children kindness, academic success, self-confidence, or something else? This reflection will inform all the decisions you make in your work as a teaching team, and it will help you align your goals for the children with your goals for the adults in your setting. Any educator will benefit from this reflection. If you are an administrator and your school already has a mission statement, do you think every teacher knows what it is? If not, what could you do to make this more visible to teachers? If you are a team leader, have you ever talked with your team about what qualities the school values? If you are on a team of teachers, do you feel your team is in line with the values of the school? Are there ways your team could make your values clearer to families?

Ultimately, the work teachers do every day is about the children. We show up, struggle, and strive to be better because we believe that teaching young children matters. If you can bring every conversation back to what is best for the child, you will make decisions with integrity. By definition, a team is a group of people working together for a shared desired outcome. Any work your team does to clarify your shared professional goals will make your team stronger and more effective. When you frequently remind yourselves of the goal you are pursuing together, and when young children's learning and well-being are at the heart of that goal, you continue to more closely align intention with action.

The following reflection will help frame your context. You can do this on your own or enlist the help of a trusted administrator or colleague.

Reflection: Define Your Setting

What kind of program are we?

What populations do we serve?

What is our mission or vision statement? If we don't have a mission or vision statement, what do we most wish for the children to gain from their experience at our program?

What makes us unique?

What are our strengths and weaknesses as an organization?

How do we offer professional development? Can we improve upon this?

What is my role in the team?

Is my role in this team supporting the mission or vision statement or desired outcomes of the program?

Tools for Administrators

If your program doesn't have an established mission or vision statement, at your next staff meeting, ask the teachers what they think the values of the organization are. If the group is large, break it up into teaching teams. (The administrative team is a separate group.) If the group is small, as in a family child care, you can do this exercise in one group.

Take turns sharing the values each group came up with and write down the words mentioned more than once, or those that are particularly striking. This activity will spark some great conversation among the teachers and lead you to what your shared values are. Hopefully it will also generate more questions for you and your colleagues to consider together.

Tie your values into the work you do with children and families. You can follow up this conversation by using the words your community chose in future conversations. If you already have agreed-upon values, are you incorporating them into the conversation as much as you can? Could every member of your staff list the values?

A Culture of Collaboration

Culture is "the beliefs, customs, arts, etc., of a particular society, group, place, or time"; it is also "the act of developing the intellectual and moral faculties especially by education" (*Merriam-Webster.com* 2016). Inherent in this definition is the idea that culture is unique to a particular society, and it is influenced by the contextual elements of place and time.

In the previous section, you spent some time defining your particular setting and figuring out what is important to your teams and families. The next question you can ask yourself is, "Can we educators shape the culture of our school for the better?"

As an educator, you know that by collaborating you can take the best of every individual to create stronger teams and stronger learning environments for young children. But how do you achieve a culture of collaboration in an

Even if you are not intentionally creating a culture in your program, a culture still exists. Silence and unspoken norms carry meaning to staff; however, individuals may interpret different meanings. Why not be deliberate and direct about your organization's culture instead?

organization? How do you create a school where all team members are invited to contribute their strengths, mistakes are seen as learning opportunities, and the team is valued over the individual? If you and your colleagues agree on a set of shared values, how do you make sure you are truly prioritizing those values in your work with children and families?

The first step in creating a culture of collaboration is to look closely at how you spend your time together as professionals. What are your meetings like? Does everyone have a voice, or do a few people do all the talking? These are some of the questions to ask yourself when you are looking closely at your school's culture. It is too easy in a school or child care setting to become entrenched in your own work, your own classroom and your own goals for children. It takes effort to think outside your own classroom and to think about the way your classroom fits into the larger picture. The time you spend thinking about how your team fits into the organization is an investment in yourself as a professional. It also demonstrates your commitment to continued education. Schools are not just places where children learn; they are places where teachers and administrators learn, too.

Tools for Administrators

Look closely at how you organize your staff meetings. Staff meetings are crucial in the development of school culture, because rarely do early childhood educators spend professional time together while not supervising children. Meetings are a time for educators to zero in on key aspects of the program. Meetings can be a time to inspire and reinvigorate one another. If your meetings are not lively and dynamic, consider restructuring how you spend this important time.

Try breaking up into small groups, or pairs, for parts of the conversation, and then sharing ideas with the larger group. Often people who are uncomfortable speaking to an entire room will share more easily with a smaller group or in pairs. This strategy gives all the chance to express their opinions to their colleagues. At the start of the year, structure conversations so that teaching teams are the small groups. This way teams will have more opportunities for dialogue and building trust. As the year progresses, you can mix up the groups to make sure teachers are building relationships outside their teams as well.

Figure out how much of your staff meeting time is spent in purposeful, professional dialogue and how much time participants spend passively listening. You can ask a staff member to observe a meeting and track what percentage of the meeting is in dialogue and who does most of the talking. If meetings are mostly passive, consider devoting some meeting time to engaging in conversation about your program, goals, and initiatives.

Place and time are defining factors of a culture. Since place and time evolve, so must we educators evolve and adapt to teach our culture to the next generation. It is by being united about your goals that you will have the most effective impact on children's learning.

You may work in a setting that is fixed in a particular mind-set. That mind-set may not feel open, transparent, and supportive. Short of finding other employment, what can you do? You can influence the culture of your school by starting reflective conversations with your team. The culture of your classroom can influence and inspire the work that others are doing in your setting. And who knows—you could start a revolution!

Reflective Practice

Reflective practice is asking questions, looking beneath the surface, and thinking deeply to refine your practice as leaders or teachers. Imagine you are looking in a mirror at your reflection. You are looking with focus and scrutinizing what you see. Sometimes you like what you see; sometimes you find things you want to change. When you and your team reflect on your teaching practice—observing, analyzing, considering, and reconceptualizing experiences—you grow as professionals (Sullivan and Glanz 2005). You can refine your practice by observing the work you have done, reflecting on the process and outcome, and making the necessary adjustments. When you reflect on your practice with your team, the possibilities for learning multiply.

If your team is a machine, with different parts of the machine working together to function smoothly, reflecting together is the maintenance of the machine. Without regular maintenance, machines break down, rust, and stop working. The same is true for teams working together day after day. Regular maintenance will keep your team running smoothly and efficiently.

The graphic at the top of page 12 illustrates the cycle of observation, reflection, and adjustment in a learning environment. (Remember, a learning environment is defined not just by the children's learning but also by the learning of teachers and families.) Your observation leads you to ask questions, which leads you to make adjustments in your teaching practice or learning environment, which then leads you back to observing to see how those adjustments affect your teaching or your learning environment.

The word *observe* in this graphic means to observe the whole learning environment: the children, the team, the relationships with families, the team's connection to the school, and the school's connection to the community. The word *reflect* means to look at what you have observed and ask questions of yourself and your team, to look closely and examine the learning environment.

The word *adjust* means to make small or large changes based on how you and your team answer the questions you ask yourselves. You complete the cycle when you observe the impact of the adjustments you and your team have made and see how they affect the whole. Then the cycle starts all over again and repeats endlessly.

OBSERVE
ADJUST
REFLECT

Asking questions is essential to the process of reflection. This book gives you and your team sample questions on a variety of topics to get your conversations started. These questions are merely a jumping-off point for you and your colleagues. Many more questions will emerge as you dive into the reflective process with your team. As human beings—and especially as educators of human beings—we are never done learning. While there will come a time when you feel confident, self-assured, and competent as an early childhood educator, there will never be a point at which you know everything. Factors such as how children learn, what families need, and what research is being done in our field are constantly evolving. When you demonstrate to your teaching team that you are curious, open, and a work in progress, you create an arena of learning where your teammates can feel safe to learn with you and from you. And what better example can you set for the young children in your care than being teachers who love to learn?

Teachers learn more → Children learn more

Engaging in this type of inquiry with your team will also create a space for you and your team members to get to know one another on a deeper level and to generate a deeper sense of your shared experience. The work you do as early childhood educators is all about fundamentals such as trust, safety, and acceptance. Reflecting together will support you and your team in defining what is fundamental about your approach to your classroom.

Team Roles in an Early Childhood Setting

Let's start our chapter on team roles by taking some time to identify your strengths. This will be your compass as you go deeper into the team reflections. It will remind you of what you bring to your team. This reflection can be done in your team meeting. Devote the first twenty or so minutes to filling out the forms individually, and then share your responses. Sometimes you will be surprised to hear what your colleagues consider your strengths, and vice versa. The Strengths Reflection is a safe place to start this work with your team because it focuses on what every team member is already doing well. This exercise will begin to build the trust necessary to share openly in your team and to grow personally and professionally.

Strengths Reflection

What are your strengths as a teacher?

What are your strengths as a team member?

What are your strengths in building trusting relationships with families?

What unique qualities do you bring to your school?

In what ways does your team rely on you?

Why do you work with children?

If you could not work with children, what would you do instead?

Leadership

Inherent in the job description of lead teacher is leadership. The lead teacher leads not only the children but also the team of adults who is working in service of the children. It's important to remember that the team serves the children, not the lead teacher. Framing the lead teacher's role as "lead advocate for children's learning" is a way to keep children always at the center of the team's work. The role of the lead teacher is to have a vision for how best to serve the children and to inspire in her team a desire to move toward that vision. This is not to say that other team members cannot exhibit leadership; in fact, part of the role of lead teacher is to recognize emerging leadership in assistants and support their growth by encouraging assistants to make meaningful contributions. The lead teacher is the visionary for the team and the one who holds the team in the frame provided by the mission and values work done earlier.

Thomas J. Sergiovanni, a leading voice in educational leadership, defines a leader as a moral steward and facilitator of connections, as opposed to the traditional definition of leader as an authoritarian who pushes and pulls members of the organization (Jossey-Bass Inc. 2000, 270). This type of leader elicits the best from teachers through team building, shared decision making, developing leadership in others, and reinforcing the value of collegiality. This type of leadership, sometimes called "servant leadership," is so called because the leader always makes decisions with the goal of making work meaningful for those doing the work.

With a servant leadership model, an early childhood setting is a learning organization, or a community of learners—and the learners include the teachers and administrators. Peter Senge, founder of the Society for Organizational Learning, defines a learning organization as an organization in which people are committed to expanding their patterns of thinking, are encouraged to think beyond boundaries, and are continually learning how to learn together (Senge 1990, 13).

This model works for a team of early childhood teachers because of the tasks we share over the course of a day in the classroom. At any time, a team member may be called upon to comfort a child, help a child meet basic needs, or mediate conflict between children. While some work falls directly to the lead teacher, enough responsibilities are shared that a more collectivist approach to running a team is appropriate.

While many different styles of leadership exist, any effective leader must possess seven virtues, according to educational leadership professor Jeffrey Glanz. Those virtues are courage, impartiality, empathy, judgment, enthusiasm, humility, and imagination (Glanz 2002). On page 16 you will find a set of reflection questions on leadership virtues for you to consider on your own or with your team. If you find that it's difficult to answer any of the questions, that's great! It means you have identified the areas you need to work on. The questions will help you focus on the areas in which you have the most potential for growth.

Team leaders are traditionally the givers of feedback. When leaders freely invite feedback, it sets an example for the team that all members are works in progress. For example, a team leader can let her team know that she is working on expressing more imagination in the classroom and invite input from her team. Team leaders could also work with other leaders in the school to complete this exercise. Perhaps all the lead teachers could attempt these questions together and talk about how leadership virtues are expressed in their own classroom environments.

Assistant teachers can use this form to examine leadership virtues, too. A teacher who is currently an assistant may find she is on a path to more leadership. Or an assistant teacher may have no desire to lead and find that she prefers to take a supportive role on the team. Regardless of the amount of leadership a teacher chooses to take on in the organization, each teacher is an important part of the team, and the virtues reflection will foster a shared vision for the team.

Reflection: Leadership Virtues

How do I exhibit courage in my work with children, my team, and my colleagues?

How do I exhibit impartiality in my work with children, my team, and my colleagues?

How do I express empathy in my work with children, my team, and my colleagues?

How do I demonstrate judgment in my work with children, my team, and my colleagues?

How do I portray enthusiasm in my work with children, my team, and my colleagues?

How do I demonstrate humility in my work with children, my team, and my colleagues?

How do I express imagination in my work with children, my team, and my colleagues?

What are the areas in which I can improve?

Is there a leader in my setting who can help me improve in these areas?

The Invisible Work of the Leader

Vietnamese Buddhist monk Thich Nhat Hanh uses the metaphor of a small boat crossing the Gulf of Thailand to describe a quality that I believe is essential in leaders. Nhat Hanh describes the many people who fled Vietnam in small boats after the war. These people often got caught in storms or rough waters. If even one person aboard stayed calm and demonstrated that sense of calm through facial expression, voice, and demeanor, then the entire boat had a better chance of surviving the journey (Nhat Hanh 1996, 12). It is that calm, peaceful quality that I call the leader's "invisible work." This work is not easy to see, but it has effects that ripple outward to touch everyone involved. The following reflection will help you define and practice this work for the benefit of your team. When you begin to practice this quality of peaceful composure, you will see the benefits to the children, to your team, and to families.

On pages 18–19 and 20–21, you will find two sets of reflective questions focused on invisible work. One is for team leaders, and the other is for assistant teachers. Your team can approach these reflections in one of two ways, depending on the degree of trust you have built in one another.

If you have built trust in your team, the team members could fill out the team leader reflection with you in mind. They could do this individually during a team meeting and then share their answers with the group. This is an opportunity to give and receive feedback within your team and take an honest look at the climate you are creating in the classroom.

If you have not yet built up that degree of trust, you can just fill out the leader reflection while assistants complete the assistant reflection, and then share all your answers as a group. This way each team member is focused on her own contributions and not neccesarily inviting feedback from others—yet. This exercise of shared self-reflection is the kind of activity that will build the trust neccesary to give honest feedback to one another.

Reflection for Team Leaders: The Invisible Work

Read through the scenario and imagine your own classroom and team, and think about how you typically respond to this type of situation.

> It's one of those days in your classroom! The weather has prevented you from taking children outside, and they are bursting with energy. Two children in your classroom seem to be pressing each other's buttons and butting heads every few minutes. Someone just knocked over a vase, and water and flowers are strewn on the floor. As you turn to get some towels, someone slips in the water and bursts into tears.

Freeze this moment to answer the following questions:

What is the expression on your face right now?

Are you moving slowly and purposefully, or are you rushing to put out fires?

What is the tone of your voice? Is it low and calm or loud and agitated?

Are you making reassuring eye contact with your team or avoiding eye contact? Or are you rolling your eyes?

Are you taking deep breaths, taking quick and shallow breaths, or holding your breath?

Is anyone responsible for these mishaps?

Are you actively modeling for your team how to respond in this type of situation?

How are you indicating what the greatest priority is in this moment?

Reflection for Assistants: The Invisible Work

Read through the scenario and imagine your own classroom and team, and think about how you typically respond to this type of situation.

> It's one of those days in your classroom! The weather has prevented you from taking children outside, and they are bursting with energy. Two children in your classroom seem to be pressing each other's buttons and butting heads every few minutes. Someone just knocked over a vase, and water and flowers are strewn on the floor. As you turn to get some towels, someone slips in the water and bursts into tears.

Freeze this moment to answer the following questions:
What is the expression on your face right now?

Are you moving slowly and purposefully, or are you rushing to put out fires?

What is the tone of your voice? Is it low and calm or loud and agitated?

Are you taking deep breaths, taking quick and shallow breaths, or holding your breath?

Who or what is the most important priority in this moment?

Do you look for direction in this moment, or do you act on instinct?

What do you need to stay calm in this type of scenario?

From *Team Teaching in Early Childhood: Leadership Tools for Reflective Practice* by Uniit Carruyo, © 2017.

Published by Redleaf Press, www.redleafpress.org. This page may be reproduced for classroom use only.

The Role of the Lead Teacher

What is the role of the lead teacher? On the surface, the role of the lead teacher is to create a learning environment for young children, develop and implement curriculum, and ensure optimum outcomes for the children in the classroom.

The role of the lead teacher goes even deeper than this. To ensure optimum outcomes for the children, the teaching team must be healthy and efficient, and the relationships with families must be trusting. The role of the lead teacher, therefore, is a trio of equally important responsibilities. In early childhood, the success of your work with children is integrally connected to the time and energy you invest in all three.

The team   The families

The children

The above figure represents the three elements of families, children, and team in balance. Part of the role of the team leader is to balance these three elements. Communicating with your team regularly will help you achieve this balance. Like any balancing act, balance in a teaching team is not a static end goal. Rather, it is a process of paying constant attention to the state of the learning environment, with many microadjustments along the way.

Working with young children is a big part of teacher training and preparation, whether that means teacher certification, education classes, or years of experience working with children. But teacher training usually does not address team teaching specifically. And yet the health of the team is integral to the tone of the classroom. The role of the lead teacher starts by acknowledging that the time spent investing in building a strong team will improve the outcomes for children and families.

Setting the Tone: The Families

As the leader of the classroom, you set the tone for staff relationships with families. It is up to you to prioritize good communication with families, model partnering with caregivers, and demonstrate how to treat child-family relationships with respect.

Here's how this looks in practice:

- Greet families warmly every day at drop-off and pickup.
- Make time to answer family members' questions or schedule a time to answer their questions in person or via phone call.
- Respond to family questions in a timely manner.

- Give families multiple ways to understand their child's day, whether by printed newsletter, report of the day, photos or anecdotes about their child's day, or classroom blog.

- Never undermine the child-family relationship—even if you disagree with their caregiving choices. While you spend many hours of the week with your students, no teacher can take the place of children's relationships with their families.

- Notice and celebrate families for the ways in which they support their children's growth and development.

- Help your team reframe difficult situations that come up and avoid judging, personalizing, or interpreting families' decisions or behaviors in a negative light. This will help your team create a more positive work environment and help strengthen the bond between home and school.

To learn and be at their best, the children in your care must first trust you. One step to building trust with children is for their families to demonstrate trust in you and the program. If family involvement or healthy relationships with families are impossible for some reason, it's still important to respect children's bonds with their families. Children are sensitive, intuitive beings, dependent on adults for their survival. They can perceive tension and judgment but cannot make sense of it. Part of making a safe space for children to learn is creating an environment free of assumptions, especially regarding their families. Regardless of what you think of family decision making, your role as an educator and a caregiver is to protect children from emotional harm and support their development.

Too often, teachers engage in a subtle form of negativity in which they do not value the role of families or they judge family choices. While not all family members are as skilled with children as early childhood teachers are, a more productive strategy is to view family members as developing individuals, similar to the children (Riley et al. 2008).

It is the challenging families in school communities who often need the teachers' patient support. When you view family members as developing in their roles, you can offer research and experientially based strategies to support their growth. You would certainly not expect a novice in any other role to be proficient at it; the same should be true for child rearing. There are no prerequisites for raising children. Meanwhile, early childhood educators do in fact have special training to teach children or years of experience working with children. Remembering that you are the first and best resource to support families in their work as caregivers will help you develop compassion and patience for them and keep your relationships with them as positive and supportive as possible. Parents and caregivers are learning as they go, and keeping this in mind will help you be supportive in your conversations.

When you demonstrate these practices as priorities, your team will follow your lead, and this will set the stage for the child's learning in your care. For families, teachers are the only connection they have to their children's school day. Young children may not have the language or memory to share details of their day with families at home. The team is the link between home and school, and the strength of that link is influenced by the tone the team sets in communication with families.

Setting the Tone: The Team

Language is something we use so much that it can be easy to overlook the influence of our language on one another. As the leader of your team, you set the tone of the classroom. Whether you are an extrovert or an introvert, funny or serious, outgoing or reserved, the language you use with your team members affects their experience. You know you are always modeling expectations for the children. Be aware that you are also always modeling expectations for the adults in your classroom. Following are examples of respectful language to use with your teammates:

1. Instead of: "Milo needs help now" or "I need you to help Milo."
    Try: "Will you please help Milo?"

2. Instead of: "We're supposed to sit with children during lunch or snacktime."
    Try: "Will you please sit with a table during lunch or snacktime? This modeling helps them learn how to sit steadily and stay on task."

3. Instead of: "We can't go home early because admin scheduled a meeting tonight."
    Try: "We're staying for a staff meeting tonight."

4. Instead of: "Well, someone got up on the wrong side of the bed!"
    Try: "Are you okay? You don't seem like your usual self today."

In examples 1 and 2, the leader is taking ownership of directives she is giving to her teammates, not hiding behind passive *supposed to*s or interpretations such as *Milo needs*. The lead teacher is asking her teammate to do something *she* thinks is important. By eliminating phrases like "I need you to," she makes the request for help about Milo's needs, not her own. Also, the lead teacher is asking—not telling—her teammates what to do. Your team always has a choice about whether to follow your lead, and your job is to help team members understand *why* you would like them to follow you. This approach demonstrates respect for what they are doing and understanding that they are operating to the best of their ability at any given time. They already know they are in a support role and that you are in charge. Using respectful language with them shows them that you value their roles and see them as meaningful contributors to the collective work.

Example 3 demonstrates not painting the administration as a common enemy. As the head of your team, you are part of the leadership of your school. If you disagree with something your administration is doing, it's part of your role as head advocate of your classroom to go directly to the person in charge and have a respectful conversation about it. Simply by belonging to an organization with flawed systems, you are part of the problem—especially if you are a senior staff member (Heifetz and Linsky 2002). Identifying the way in which you perpetuate the problems you face is key to being an effective advocate in your organization and for your team. An integral part of your role as leader in your classroom is to create a reassuring tone for your team. They look to you as an example, and when you participate in a drama that puts your team at odds with leadership, you chip away at the culture of the school rather than build it up and strengthen it.

Tools for the Team

Agree on a set of nonverbal signs you can use to communicate with one another across a crowded classroom. A handful of American Sign Language (ASL) signs, such as those that follow, can go a long way in building camaraderie in your team and helping you communicate quickly with one another, while maintaining a calm tone in the room:

Be right back.
I need a bathroom break.
Help, please.
Thank you.
Look at this.
I'll tell you later.

In example 4, the leader keeps her concern for her teammate at the forefront of the conversation, rather than putting her teammate on the defensive by making assumptions about her state of mind. This gives the teammate the chance to respond, for example, "Yes, I would feel much better if I could grab a quick cup of coffee," and in this way, avoid unnecessary conflict or stress due to a problem that can be fixed easily.

Here's where you can find more signs that you might be able to use: http://commtechlab.msu.edu/sites/aslweb/browser.htm

CLASSROOM SIGN LANGUAGE

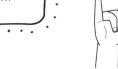

The letter *I*
Used to show that you have a **question**.
("**I** have a question.")

The letter *A*
Used to show that you have an **answer**.

The letter *C*
Used to show that you have a **comment**.

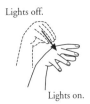

Lights off.

Lights on.

May I use the restroom?

One moment, please.

That was off-topic.

I am ignoring you.
(student-to-student)

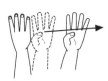

Line up, please.

volunteer

May I get a drink?

Thank you.

Stand up.

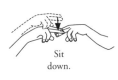

Sit down.

Pencils down.

Setting the Tone: The Children

The third and most important way a lead teacher sets the tone in an organization is through her work with the children. Early childhood educators come to this work because they love children. No one comes to this work for a high salary, accolades, or social status. We do this work because we love children and believe that devoting our careers to their education is a valuable use of our time. We believe, as Maria Montessori says, "the child is both a hope and a promise for mankind" (Montessori 1972). Knowing that this is what brings most people to the field of early childhood education, we must reflect on what impression we give our team in the work we do with children.

Every time we interact with a child, we set an example for our team. If you are disrespectful toward children, this attitude is contagious, just as positivity and compassion are contagious. Following is a set of questions to ask yourself about the way in which you communicate with children. Try devoting one of your team meetings to this reflection. Allow twenty minutes at the beginning of your meeting to fill out the form individually, and then share your responses with your team for the next thirty minutes. If this kind of self-reflection is new to you, it will take some practice to step back and look at yourself objectively. Remember your strengths from the exercise at the beginning of this chapter (page 13), and keep in mind that to grow and become a stronger teacher, you have to bend and stretch.

Reflection:
Setting the Tone for the Team: Working with Children

What happens in my classroom when a child falls apart, whether the problem is missing a caregiver, having wet pants, or being overly tired or hungry? Do I model care and compassion by meeting the needs of this child, or do I let one of my teammates handle it?

When a child presents behavioral challenges for my classroom, do I set a tone of compassion and sensitivity? Do I roll my eyes, sigh, or become exasperated?

Do I fight for children in my classroom by adjusting my teaching style, changing the environment, or spending more time with them, or am I quick to pass them off as unmanageable?

Do I dig deeper for the sake of a child with challenging behaviors by soliciting more information from the child's family or other experts?

From *Team Teaching in Early Childhood: Leadership Tools for Reflective Practice* by Uniit Carruyo, © 2017.

Published by Redleaf Press, www.redleafpress.org. This page may be reproduced for classroom use only.

Do I complain about the children with my team or allow my team to complain about the children?

Do I genuinely enjoy being with the children? Do I laugh and smile with them every day?

Do I rush children?

Do I talk to children with the same amount of respect I use to talk with adults?

From *Team Teaching in Early Childhood: Leadership Tools for Reflective Practice* by Uniit Carruyo, © 2017.

Published by Redleaf Press, www.redleafpress.org. This page may be reproduced for classroom use only.

The Role of the Assistant

The role of the assistant is, by definition, a supportive role. While the work is collaborative, and every team member carries responsibility for the whole, the assistant supports the vision of the lead teacher. All the tone setting discussed in this section applies to every member of the team, without the responsibility of leading. For some teachers, this is the sweet spot for teaching in a team. Assistant teachers get to be with children and do the work of early childhood without having the weight of leadership. For some teachers, being an assistant is a step on the path toward leadership. Either way, learning to communicate with one's team, express one's needs and opinions, and give meaningful contributions is essential for the health of the team.

Following is a reflection specifically for assistant teachers. The purpose of the reflection is to clarify the assistant teacher's role so that she can communicate better with the team and contribute meaningfully. The reflection is intended for teachers to do on their own and use as a guide for communicating with their team.

Tools for Teams

Encourage one another to practice mindful presence during the workday by keeping a small box with a lid for each team member with a note inside that says, "Place worries here." Encourage one another to leave troubles in the box before entering the classroom so that each team member can be at her best for the children during the workday. Teachers can also put something personal in their boxes that reminds them to be fully present—a stone, a picture, or any other meaningful item. Everyone has bad days, and this is a way to make a habit of taking a moment before entering the classroom to pause, breathe, and put personal worries aside for the day. This also encourages camaraderie through a shared experience and reinforces the mission of the team: creating an environment where children's well-being and learning are the focus.

Reflection: The Role of the Assistant

What are your responsibilities in the classroom?

What are you contributing to the classroom that is unique to you?

Does the lead teacher have a clear vision for the classroom that you support?

If not, what would you like to see change?

What do you consider the lead teacher's strengths?

Do you feel the communication in your team is clear and healthy? If not, why not?

Do you feel your classroom is an optimal learning environment for children? Why or why not?

What do you think your team is doing well?

What do you think your team could improve?

Do you feel comfortable giving feedback to the lead teacher? If not, why not?

From *Team Teaching in Early Childhood: Leadership Tools for Reflective Practice* by Uniit Carruyo, © 2017.
Published by Redleaf Press, www.redleafpress.org. This page may be reproduced for classroom use only.

Teamwork in Action: Communication Strategies

T he day-to-day interactions we have in our teams are opportunities to both lead and listen more effectively. Even simple exchanges of information can become complicated when we are supervising young children and juggling competing priorities. This chapter breaks down communication into various components so we can look closely at how we listen to our teammates and at how our communication affects one another in the classroom.

Ask Questions

Being a member of a team or leading a team is not always about taking decisive action and initiating reform. Just as often, it is about stepping back, observing, and asking questions. Asking more questions is a simple way to problem solve and work together. When a team member has a complaint or concern, spend some time asking questions before you respond or offer solutions.

Take a look at the following dialogues to see how using questions can help you communicate with a teammate and prevent misunderstandings. Here is a scenario in which the lead teacher (LT) does not ask questions of the assistant teacher (AT):

AT: Hey, can we talk?

LT: Uh-oh, you look upset.

AT: I'm so frustrated with Diane. I feel like every time I'm working with a student, she micromanages me.

LT: Yeah, I've noticed that happens.

AT: I know! And I feel really undermined in front of the children. I would never do that to her, and she does it all the time.

LT: Well, maybe you should talk directly to her about it.

AT: Okay....

In this scenario, the conversation ends, and the assistant teacher still feels mad and frustrated. When she confronts her colleague, she carries with her that frustration and puts her colleague on the defensive. There is little chance of a successful, productive resolution to the problem.

Here is the same problem with the lead teacher using questions as a tool:

AT: Hey, can we talk?

LT: Sure, what's going on?

AT: I'm so frustrated with Diane. I feel like every time I'm working with a student, she micromanages me.

LT: Can you give me an example?

AT: Well…(*thinking*)…today, for example, when I was helping Alex with his math, Diane leaned over and told him it was time to clean up, just when he was about to work out the problem on his own.

LT: So, you were working with Alex, and he almost had the problem solved, and Diane interrupted to tell him it was time to clean up?

AT: Yes.

LT: (*validating*) I can see how that would feel frustrating.

AT: Yes, it was.

LT: Do you think Diane knows she upset you?

AT: Well, no, I guess not.

LT: Do you think that if you talked to her, she would understand?

AT: Um…yeah, I think if I told her it made me uncomfortable, she would understand.

LT: Do you feel comfortable telling her that it felt like an interruption, and that maybe there is another way to let him know it's time to clean up? Maybe a sign or hand on the shoulder?

AT: Yeah, maybe I'll ask her just to tap me on the shoulder, and then I can finish up and let Alex know it's time to clean up.

LT: I agree—Diane will be open to doing that. I'll do that, too. I like that idea.

AT: Okay!

In this scenario, the assistant teacher walks away feeling heard and having a tool for solving the problem. She can approach Diane in a nondefensive way. This approach also focuses on what the assistant teacher is experiencing concretely, rather than spending time on assumptions or interpretations.

Offer a New Perspective

A powerful thing you can offer your team is a new perspective. In the above scenario, the lead teacher could also offer her team member some insight into what Diane might be feeling. For example, she could say, "I know how worried Diane is about Alex, so she was probably acting out of concern, and she didn't think about how that might make you feel. What do you think about that?" This gives the upset assistant teacher a chance to think compassionately about Diane, and it softens the upset. Early childhood teachers usually have big, loving hearts—it's why we do the work we do with children. Applying the love we so easily give children to adults, who may feel more challenging or threatening to us, takes practice.

When a lead teacher reminds an assistant teacher that there may be another perspective and reassures her that her colleague is most likely acting out of her commitment to children, the lead teacher gives a reminder that all team members are doing the same work for the same reasons. Team members have to practice thinking of one another as allies and not competitors. The goal for a team leader is to support the team members in approaching conflict with more compassion and less emotional reaction, not to sweep conflict under the rug or handle it for them.

As a leader, part of what you bring to your team is a view of the big picture. The more leadership you take on, the more perspectives you must consider. If you have knowledge or information about other people or other parts of the program, you can use that insight to foster connections among your team members that they may not have known were possible. All team members share equally in the responsibility to give one another clear and direct feedback, to ask for clarity on roles and goals, to listen compassionately, to have empathy for one another, and to trust that every member is doing her best.

Reframe the Situation

In any conflict, we have the option to assume best intentions. Leaders, in particular, have more responsibility to model constructive problem solving. Reframing situations like the one described on page 34 in a more positive light can empower team members to do the same for themselves and one another. This tool can transform ego-based emotions like defensiveness and embarrassment into compassion and empathy.

An interesting concept called Occam's razor is helpful here. Medieval English philosopher William of Occam stated that *pluralitas non est ponenda sine necessitate*, "plurality should not be posited without necessity" (Duignan 2015). The principle means that of two competing theories, the simpler explanation is preferred. In other words, the simplest explanation is usually the right one. We can apply this concept to our reframing process by making as few assumptions as possible when we encounter a problem. By doing so, we support not only the health of our team but also our own sense of equilibrium.

Following is a reflection to help you and your team practice the skill of reframing. This can be a fun exercise to do in pairs in a team meeting and then share with the group. Think about Occam's razor as you answer. For each scenario, pick the answer that best describes you, and then practice reframing the situation with your partner or team. You can also make up some scenarios that would be typical for you at your school and then trade scenarios with your partner. The idea is to think outside any reflexive reactions you might have and to try to lighten up your outlook on these everyday situations.

Reframing Reflection

You arrive at school in a great mood. You bounce into the classroom to find your teammate quietly preparing for the day. You say, "Good morning!" She mumbles a reply but does not look up from her task or make eye contact. What is your first thought or response?

1. You think your teammate must be mad at you, and your mind starts to race with what you might have done to elicit this rude response. The good mood you were in disappears. Now you feel offended.

2. You think your teammate must have had a hard morning at home. You ask her gently if she is okay and if she would like to talk about anything. Then you let it go and think, "She will talk when she's ready, and it most likely has nothing to do with me."

3. You ask your teammate if she's okay, and if she doesn't respond in a friendly way, you worry you have upset her. You spend the rest of the day walking on eggshells.

4. You react some other way. (Briefly describe it.)

A parent is rushing to drop off his child in the morning. You overhear him talking quickly to his toddler and sighing with exasperation at how slowly his child is moving. The child keeps getting distracted by things on the way to the classroom, and you see the look of impatience on the father's face. He meets your eye and frowns. What is your first thought or response?

1. This parent is too hard on his child. He should not have had kids in the first place! You give him a stern eye and speak only to the child as they arrive.

2. You think, "This parent must be very worried about getting somewhere on time," smile at both of them, and offer to help the child so the parent can go.

3. You think this parent is being rude to you and wonder what you did to offend him. You act polite but curt toward him.

4. You react some other way. (Briefly describe it.)

Write your own scenario:

1.

2.

3.

4.

From *Team Teaching in Early Childhood: Leadership Tools for Reflective Practice* by Uniit Carruyo, © 2017.

Published by Redleaf Press, www.redleafpress.org. This page may be reproduced for classroom use only.

Now that you have taken some time to practice reframing situations with your team, here is a reflection to see how well you listen to one another. This reflection is for you to do on your own.

Reflection: Are You Listening?

You can offer your teammates every opportunity to be heard with an open mind free of judgment. How do you know you are listening with an open mind? Next time one of your team members comes to you with a concern, take a moment to notice your physical and emotional response.

- Do you tense up, expecting the worst?
- Do you cross your arms or legs or avoid eye contact?
- Do you hold your breath or breathe faster?
- Do you tune in and out of what your colleague is saying, while your mind races with ways to defend yourself or with quick fixes for the problem?
- Do you interrupt, or do you wait for your colleague to finish speaking?

If you answer any of these with a "yes," then you may not really be listening.

From *Team Teaching in Early Childhood: Leadership Tools for Reflective Practice* by Uniit Carruyo, © 2017.
Published by Redleaf Press, www.redleafpress.org. This page may be reproduced for classroom use only.

If you found that you might not really be listening, that's okay, because listening is a skill you can practice. Once you get more comfortable with this kind of listening, it will be a powerful tool for you and your team. Next time one of your team members approaches you with a concern, tune in and become aware of your body language. Stay open—mentally and physically—and breathe to remind yourself to stay in the moment with your colleague. Try listening without thinking of solutions or defenses. When your colleague says something, paraphrase what she said and repeat it back to her to make sure you really understand the issue. Most of the time, the issue isn't personal, and you can offer a positive reframing of the situation for her or help her think outside the box to come up with solutions.

The listening reflection can help you tune in to what you experience when a teammate tries to communicate with you. You can use this reflection to be more attentive when you are listening and to practice the skill of listening without ego.

Using listening phrases takes a little practice, but soon this technique will become second nature, and the benefits will be worth the effort. Most of the time, people just want to be heard, and that alone makes them feel better. You offer your team something valuable when you simply offer them your concentrated attention. Your team members will feel more valued when they see you are really listening, you will build more trust within your team, and your team will have a more relaxed and easy tone.

> Here are a few useful phrases to practice when you are listening:
> - "So, I hear you saying that..."
> - "It sounds like you feel that..."
> - "What I heard you say was.... Is that right?"

Focus on Interests

Whenever conflict arises, Harvard Negotiation Project founders Roger Fisher, William Ury, and Bruce Patton advise focusing on interests, not positions, to reach resolution. The interest is the silent motivation behind the position someone takes in a conflict. It usually has to do with basic human needs. To highlight the difference between interests and positions, Fisher, Ury, and Patton give the example of two men arguing in a library. One wants the window open; the other wants the window closed. When the librarian asks them to say why they want it open or closed, one says, "For fresh air," and the other replies, "To avoid a draft." Fresh air and draft avoidance are the interests behind the positions, which are the window being open or closed. After the librarian identifies the interests, she comes up with a solution that satisfies both interests by opening a window in the next room, providing fresh air without a draft (Fisher, Ury, and Patton 1991).

Following is another example from my setting. The teachers wanted administrators to stop delivering messages about staffing, therapists, or family communication during the school day. The teachers found it disruptive to classroom focus when the phones were ringing and messengers were walking in and out. Their interest was to reduce distraction. As administrators, our interest was to get information to the teachers about staffing and to make sure families and therapists could get information to the teachers in a timely fashion. If we had focused on positions, we would have been at an impasse. Instead, we looked at interests and came up with a solution in which administrators deliver messages via notes teachers can read in a quiet moment, and classroom phone calls occur only for urgent matters.

When we focus on interests, we demonstrate respect for one another's basic needs, rather than getting caught up in superficial conflicts. A clear way of identifying these fundamental needs is through the work of social psychologist Abraham Maslow. In his work, Maslow defines basic human needs with the following diagram:

Self-actualization
Morality, creativity, spontaneity, acceptance, purpose, meaning, and inner potential

Self-esteem
Confidence, achievement, respect of others, the need to be a unique individual

Love and belonging
Friendship, family, intimacy, sense of connection

Safety and security
Health, employment, property, family and social stability

Physiological needs
Breathing, food, water, shelter, clothing, sleep

Whether a conflict is happening with your teammates, families, or children, by identifying their basic needs, you can get to the heart of the matter quickly. Something that looks like a conflict about planning time or classroom management or interpersonal differences might actually be about feeling accepted or trust or fear.

When you get to the heart of people's concerns, you can facilitate solutions that keep multiple parties feeling heard. Sometimes the interests are shared; sometimes they are divergent. To facilitate compromise, you must identify both shared and unshared interests. When individuals come to you with concerns, they often have their individual interests in mind. Your job as a team leader is to advocate for the interests of the group, which sometimes don't dovetail perfectly with the interests of individuals. It's important that assistant teachers or team members know their interests are valued and considered in decision making for the team or classroom.

What does focusing on interests look like in an early childhood setting? Take a moment to think about your own program. What are the problems that come up regularly? In the following paragraphs, I will offer a sample conflict as an exercise in defining interests and a reflection to help you think through similar scenarios in your own setting and practice identifying interests.

Jamie is the classroom teacher of a two-year-old boy named Duane during the school day. Jamie is also one of Duane's after-school teachers. Duane is toilet training. Jamie knows Duane and his cues well and has a system for supporting his efforts. Jamie trusts that Duane will listen to his body's cues in the after-school program, just as he does during the school day. Jamie wants Duane to be able to choose to go to the bathroom. Jamie comes to you with the complaint that one of the other after-school teachers, Elena, is interfering with Duane's toilet training system by asking him repeatedly to go to the bathroom, asking if he needs to go, or checking his pants.

Let's break down this scenario into positions:

JAMIE'S POSITION Jamie wants to follow through with the thoughtful system she has come up with to support Duane. She wants to give him the space to be successful by watching him and intervening only if he seems to be putting off going to the bathroom.

ELENA'S POSITION Elena wants to make sure Duane does not have an accident during the after-school program, so she tries to prevent this by frequently reminding him to go to the bathroom and checking his pants.

Now, to dig below the surface of the conflict, let's identify the reasons behind each position:

JAMIE'S REASONS Jamie wants Duane to initiate his own bathroom visits to ensure that Duane learns to recognize his body's cues, practices good self-care, and feels successful. Jamie does not want Elena to initiate Duane's trips to the bathroom because Jamie trusts Duane to do this successfully. Jamie also feels she knows Duane best and should be able to make the call.

ELENA'S REASONS Elena wants to remind Duane to go to the bathroom to make sure he doesn't wet his pants. Elena does not want to stop reminding him, because if he does wet his pants, it could discourage him and will also make a mess she will have to clean up.

Now, let's identify the hidden interest in each position, keeping in mind Maslow's hierarchy of basic human needs:

JAMIE'S INTEREST Jamie's interest could be love and belonging or self-esteem. Jamie loves Duane and has invested a lot in his care. She wants him to be successful and feel good about himself. Jamie also wants to be regarded professionally by her colleague. She feels it is a gesture of disrespect for Elena to intervene in the system Jamie uses to care for Duane. She trusts Duane and believes he is capable of making this choice for himself and meeting his physiological needs.

ELENA'S INTEREST Elena's interest may be addressing physiological needs by trying to prevent Duane from wetting his pants and keeping the classroom dry. She sees this as a way of caring for Duane. Her interest may also be self-esteem, in that she wants to be seen as a proactive contributor to her workplace.

Finally, let's identify any shared interests:

• Both teachers want Duane to learn to use the toilet.
• Both teachers want to preserve their own self-esteem and Duane's self-esteem.
• Both teachers are doing their best.

Now, let's suggest three different solutions that respond to the interests of both positions. This is a good time to refer back to the organization's vision and mission statement or the team's shared purpose.

SOLUTION 1 Suggest that Jamie talk with Elena about how Jamie feels when Elena intervenes with Duane's school routine, emphasizing to Elena that it feels like professional respect to support her in keeping Duane's routines consistent.

SOLUTION 2 Suggest that Jamie reassure Elena that Jamie will take responsibility for cleaning up after Duane.

SOLUTION 3 Suggest that Elena and Jamie meet to discuss the routines Duane follows during the day and agree on a written behavior plan so they have clarity about what the expectations are for all parties.

Finally, we can frame the conflict in a positive light and address both teachers' basic needs by reassuring Jamie that Elena has Duane's best interests in mind, and vice versa. We can reassure both teachers that they are valuable contributors to the program and that their opinions matter, while recognizing that both want to be treated with respect.

Through exercises like examining and discussing the Jamie-and-Elena conflict, you and your team can practice stepping back to see conflicts from multiple angles. Team leaders, in particular, must be able to see situations in three dimensions. Identifying positions, focusing on interests, acting with compassion based on true needs, and positive reframing are all skills that can help you facilitate compromise in your team and your organization.

Tools for the Team

Take every opportunity to reinforce to your team that all members are doing the best they can at any given moment, and that when misunderstandings happen, a positive solution is always possible. This is true in working with families, children, and colleagues. Positivity and negativity are both contagious, so why not choose to spread positivity?

Reflection: Interests versus Positions

Describe in a few sentences or less a conflict you have had in the workplace.

Break down the conflict into positions, identifying the positions by the people who held them.

Write the outcomes the parties were hoping for and the basic needs of each party.

Find the hidden interests for each party.

Identify any shared interests.

Propose two to three solutions with shared interests as the goals.

Reframe the conflict, addressing the basic needs of each party.

From *Team Teaching in Early Childhood: Leadership Tools for Reflective Practice* by Uniit Carruyo, © 2017.
Published by Redleaf Press, www.redleafpress.org. This page may be reproduced for classroom use only.

Foundational Elements of an Effective Classroom Team

Now that we have defined what reflective leadership is in early childhood settings and have talked about basic communication strategies, let's take a close look at the seven foundational elements of a healthy team.

1. Clarity of roles
2. Meaningful contributions
3. Group norms
4. Trust
5. Common language
6. Peaceful conflict
7. Professional development

Clarity of Roles

Clarity of roles refers to an agreed-upon definition and understanding of what each team member's role is. If your program has written job descriptions, refer to them as a jumping-off point. If your program does not have written job descriptions, that's okay; you can still outline your roles with your teammates. Often programs have generalized job descriptions that leave room for imagination. This can be an advantage because it allows each team to be dynamic, just as each group of children in any given year forms a unique dynamic. Part of the team leader's role is to individualize the roles for her particular team. Each team is a living being, and no single set of rules can ensure team success. If teams incorporate the seven foundational elements of a healthy team, they can be successful in their own way by maximizing the potential of each individual.

Following is a sample of the job description for a lead infant teacher at our Montessori setting. (Note: Nido is a common name for a Montessori infant program. *Nido* is the Italian word for "nest." IMS stands for Ithaca Montessori School.)

Infant Lead Teacher Job Description

We nurture the spirit of each child through meaningful connections with families and our dedication to the principles of Montessori education.

IMS Core Values

LOVE We serve others with kindness and compassion.

RESPECT We appreciate the innate dignity of each person.

INTEGRITY We act in ways that promote trust and accountability.

PEACE We build harmony among our community.

EXCELLENCE We model high standards and a lifelong commitment to learning.

Position:	Nido Head Teacher
Reports to:	Program Director
Work schedule:	40 hours per week / 10 months per year

Family relationships/communication

- initiate communication with new family (welcome letter/meeting)
- schedule/conduct home visits
- design individualized phase-in plan
- individualize phase-in plan for every child
- maintain communication (point person, daily reports)
- hold conferences (6-week check-in, 12-month conference, transition conference, as needed)
- write narrative reports (at least once per year plus final summary)
- compile information and photos for Diarios
- check e-mail daily and respond to parent questions
- coordinate parent hour
- oversee monthly point person surveys
- warmly greet families at drop-off and pickup
- maintain and update Nido E-bulletin board
- report concerns or special circumstances with families or family communication
- be available to meet with parents as necessary
- communicate IMS values, mission, and policies in a courteous and compassionate manner

Parent education

- update photo blog at least once a month
- communicate by monthly newsletters and updates about classroom routines/schedule

Children

- maintain infant feeding schedules
- maintain diapering/introducing developmentally appropriate independence
- maintain NYS safety ratios
- implement developmentally appropriate curriculum
- handle children gently and with respect
- maintain records of children in care (documentation)
- ensure that children are signed in/out daily
- ensure that wellness logs are maintained
- submit OCFS paperwork weekly to director
- report promptly any child with special needs to IMS Child Guidance Team

Team leadership

- schedule and facilitate bimonthly meetings
- train new teachers in conjunction with program director
- supervise teaching team
- do biweekly check-ins with team members (20 minutes 1:1)
- give and receive feedback to and from team members
- liaise with program director about professional development needs of the group
- train team in NYS safety regulations
- ensure that team members take state-mandated breaks
- ensure that subs in the classroom are welcomed and oriented to classroom systems

Environmental design

- design dynamic learning environment consistent with Montessori standards
- adjust and individualize learning environment as needed to meet the needs of the group
- maintain environment according to program standards (i.e., infant/toddler consistency, primary consistency)
- keep learning environment free of clutter
- keep classroom storage areas clean and orderly (closets, cupboards, etc.)
- create systems for parents and children in the classroom (work drawers, nap bins, extra clothes, cubbies, etc.)
- keep environment clean with daily sweeping and disinfecting of surfaces

Curriculum development
- know and adhere to NYS safety regulations
- oversee classroom budget, track purchases, and document according to IMS protocol
- research and request curriculum materials as needed from program director
- regularly change learning materials in the classroom environment
- provide children with group learning opportunities as well as 1:1 lessons
- make learning materials as needed for classrooms

Interprogram collaboration
- design and implement one interprogram initiative with a classroom outside your certified level (Roots of Empathy, Reading Buddies, Montessori Mentor)

Program obligations
- fulfill requirements as outlined in offer letter of employment

Professional development
- meet annual continuing education requirements for NYS (30 hours per two-year cycle for any employee working more than 20 hours/week)
- meet annual continuing education requirements for American Montessori Society (for Montessori credential issued on or after July 1, 2013, 50 hours per five-year cycle; see AMSHQ.org for guidelines)
- participate in observations, pre- and post-observation conferences, and ongoing self-evaluation to maintain effective teaching practice

Mentorship
For teachers who have at least five years of teaching experience at IMS
- mentor a Montessori intern for the duration of their internship year
- supervise and support the internship with regular feedback
- liaise with program director about internship

Code of conduct/IMS community
- respect student confidentiality
- cooperate and problem solve with colleagues
- share resources with colleagues
- attend and participate in school functions or parent education per your offer letter

Sounds like a tough job, right? It is a tough job! Luckily, we teach in teams. While it's the lead teacher's job to ensure that the things in her job description happen, that does not mean that it's her job to do every single task herself. The expectation that every team member will make reasonable, meaningful contributions is necessary for a healthy, functioning team. Take a moment to define the roles of your team using the following reflections.

Reflection: Lead Teacher Role and Responsibilities

What are my responsibilities to the children in my classroom regarding…
safety (state guidelines, school guidelines)?

learning outcomes (curriculum, goals)?

emotional growth and development?

physical growth and development?

From *Team Teaching in Early Childhood: Leadership Tools for Reflective Practice* by Uniit Carruyo, © 2017.

Published by Redleaf Press, www.redleafpress.org. This page may be reproduced for classroom use only.

What are my responsibilities to families regarding...

communication?

curriculum?

family education?

What are my responsibilities to classroom teachers regarding...
communication?

support?

feedback?

What are my responsibilities to my program regarding...
professional development?

collaboration with colleagues?

participation in and enhancement of curriculum?

Reflection: Assistant Teacher Roles and Responsibilities

What are my responsibilities to the children in my classroom regarding…
safety (state guidelines, school guidelines)?

learning outcomes (curriculum, goals)?

emotional growth and development?

physical growth and development?

What are my responsibilities to the families regarding…
communication?

curriculum?

family education?

From *Team Teaching in Early Childhood: Leadership Tools for Reflective Practice* by Uniit Carruyo, © 2017.

Published by Redleaf Press, www.redleafpress.org. This page may be reproduced for classroom use only.

What are my responsibilities to the lead teacher regarding…
communication?

support?

feedback?

What are my responsibilities to my program regarding…
professional development?

collaboration with colleagues?

participation in and enhancement of curriculum?

Meaningful Contributions

Fostering meaningful contributions means taking the time to understand each of your team members as individuals so that each can contribute to the best of her ability. Each classroom forms its own unique dynamic, shaped by the personalities that make up the teaching team. In this section, you will find a set of reflective questions for you and each of your teammates to fill out together during a team meeting. I recommend answering these questions individually and then sharing the answers out loud with one another.

Through this exercise, you will discover your teammates' hidden talents. Often each individual's talents can be incorporated into the classroom curriculum to enrich the children's experiences. This is a win-win strategy: young children benefit from a diversified curriculum, and team members feel valued for who they are and for their unique talents. Invite a musician on the team to share music once a week at circle time. Invite an artist on the team to do an art project once a week with the children. Invite a juggler on the team to give juggling lessons to the children during gross-motor time.

This kind of thinking will lead to all kinds of positive possibilities for your classroom curriculum, including modeling camaraderie, celebrating the individual, and encouraging a spirit of mutual respect. Not only will the children benefit from this kind of thinking, but all team members will find their work more meaningful and therefore more satisfying. In early childhood education, high salaries are nonexistent. Finding the work meaningful and satisfying is what keeps us going. Highlighting one another's strengths and incorporating them in our work are steps toward increased satisfaction.

Reflection: Meaningful Contributions

Why did you choose to work in early childhood?

Why did you choose to work in this particular program?

What are your favorite things about working with young children?

What are the hardest aspects of working with young children?

What would you be if you weren't an early childhood teacher?

Name three things you love to do besides working with children.

The above questions are meant to draw very personalized answers. These answers can get you started on bringing pieces of every team member's personality to the classroom. How can your team members contribute on a professional level? To define team members' professional contributions, step back and look at all the little details it takes to make your classroom run efficiently. With some teams, the division of responsibilities may seem effortless and easy. Other teams require a more structured approach. A sample list of responsibilities might look like the following.

Willow Room Jobs

Morning

snack preparation

works: straighten, refill, put out new, order, etc.

white board

circle tone keeper

worktime tone keeper

work observation

lessons (3 period)

music with Linda participation

health log

photos

toddler reports

diapering

sign-in book

Naptime

closet: keep tidy, free of clutter

white board

load dishwasher

start dishwasher

sanitize dish tubs

wash and sanitize place mats

wash and sanitize cart

wash and sanitize counters and faucets

sweep floor

wash and sanitize table and chairs

restock diapers/wipes

toddler reports

snack preparation

check and print e-mails (admin, updates, etc.)

answer parent e-mails

works: straighten, refill, put out new, etc.

Afternoon

diapering

logs

bleach nap mats

circle

Teams can tailor the list of responsibilities to suit their vision for the classroom. Lead teachers can initiate this work and have team members choose a job for one to two months, a semester, several weeks, or whatever works for their particular team. Some team members may be eager to lead activities with the children or to be in contact with families; some may prefer to work more behind the scenes. There is no one right way of delineating responsibilities, but being clear and having a plan can prevent confusion and conflicts within the team.

Group Norms

Ideally, your team should establish group norms at the beginning of your work together. Revisit norms when a new member joins the group and when there is a new beginning on the calendar, such as the start of the school year or summer program. The norms your team generates will provide the unique framework for the basic operations of the team. Norms are partially directed by the leader of the team and partially dictated by the specific individuals who make up the team. For example, if a team member is deaf in one ear, one of the group norms may be "always make eye contact when speaking" so that this team member can read lips.

Here are some examples of group norms:

- Speak softly in the classroom to help maintain a peaceful tone.
- Use nonverbal communication in the classroom to avoid disrupting the children's concentration.
- Walk slowly in the classroom, and model this type of thoughtful movement for the children.

- Unless safety is at stake, save talking with team members for the end of the day or a time after the children have left the room.
- Speak from your own point of view with phrases like "I feel," "I think," rather than "you always" or "you do/don't" (known as "I" statements).
- Always assume that your team members have the best intentions.
- Don't take things personally.
- Ask questions when you are confused about why a team member does something rather than guessing or assuming.

These sample norms are just a starting point. You and your team can determine what is best for your classroom and your group using the following exercise. You can do this exercise at a team meeting when every member is present. The lead teacher facilitates and makes sure every team member contributes to the list. The questions will lead you to what your team's norms are. The team can brainstorm these questions together, make lists, and then pare down the lists to the core norms everyone agrees are the most important. Post them as a visual reminder of your shared agreements, add to them as the year progresses, and refine them annually.

Reflection: Group Norms

List at least ten essential elements of your ideal classroom.

What do you consider the essential elements of collaboration in a team?

What are your pet peeves in a classroom setting?

From *Team Teaching in Early Childhood: Leadership Tools for Reflective Practice* by Uniit Carruyo, © 2017.
Published by Redleaf Press, www.redleafpress.org. This page may be reproduced for classroom use only.

Tools for Teams

Consider having an annual book club with your team. Reading and discussing books about personal growth, child development, or education can strengthen your bond as a team and hone your areas of strength. For example, maybe your team has a shared passion for social justice, or arts education, or science and technology. Discovering these strengths will create areas of opportunity for learning in your team and organization.

Here are some examples of books that spark conversation on personal growth:

- *The Four Agreements* by Don Miguel Ruiz
- *The Power of Vulnerability* by Brené Brown
- *True Refuge* by Tara Brach
- *The Art of Happiness* by Dalai Lama and Howard Cutler

Here are some books that spark conversation on education:

- *The Fifth Discipline* by Peter M. Senge
- *Experience and Education* by John Dewey
- *The Absorbent Mind* by Maria Montessori

If a book club feels too ambitious, start small and just read an article with your team. Devote ten minutes during one of your team meetings to reading the article together, and then invite conversation. To keep it relevant and productive, remember to ground the conversation in the context of your setting.

Trust

Trust may be the single most important element of a healthy team. Why is it number four on the list of foundational elements? Because the first three elements are necessary for trust to develop within your team. Clearly defined roles, meaningful contributions, and group norms are the first steps to establishing a team that trusts you and one another. It's not enough for your team to trust you—they must also trust one another in order to carry out the team's duties productively. Trust is an accepted belief in one another's earnest intentions, a sense of safety in vulnerability, a belief that one will be accepted—warts and all—and a belief that others in the team genuinely care about each individual's well-being.

How do you build trust with your team? I suspect you are already very good at building trust with young children in your classroom. How did you build that trust? Perhaps you used the following strategies:

- greeting them warmly every day
- listening to them
- having realistic expectations
- being patient with them as they learn
- encouraging their growth
- allowing them to shine and be successful
- prodding them gently out of their comfort zone sometimes
- respecting them
- loving them, especially when they fall or fail

If you do all these things with young children, you already have the skills necessary to build trust with your team members. The ingredients necessary for trust don't change in adulthood; they only become more complicated because of the fears, anxieties, doubts, and worries that come with adulthood. As adults, we carry these fears and worries with us, and they act together as a lens through which we see the actions and intentions of other adults. As teachers, we know how to get the best from young children: by looking at them through a lens of kindness, optimism, and care. If we can use that same lens for viewing the adults with whom we work, we can get the best from them, too.

For example, when you are building trust with children, do you do the following?

- take their actions personally
- act in a passive-aggressive way by giving them the silent treatment when they make a mistake
- become resentful when they are very good at something or experience success
- imagine they are thinking negative thoughts about you
- act warmly some days and unapproachable on other days
- talk about them behind their backs, or negatively

Of course you don't do these things. Most early childhood teachers would never think to act this way with young children. Yet they fall into some of these destructive habits with their team members.

When team members trust one another, the individuals on the team gain the confidence to stretch and try new things. Trust encourages professional risk taking. The quality that separates good teachers from great ones is risk taking (Brazeau 2005). Having the courage and confidence to try something, even though it might fail, leads to the discoveries that create the most dynamic learning environments for young children. Here are some examples of risks team members have shared with me over the years:

1. "I can't sing. I'm afraid to lead circle time!"
2. "I'd like to take a class on something, but I'm intimidated to go back to school at my age."
3. "I get nervous when parents are watching me in the classroom. I'm afraid they are judging me."
4. "I'd like to take on more responsibility—like writing a classroom newsletter, blog, or other communication—but I'm not great with technology."

Here are some "safety nets" you could offer teammates who express such risks:

1. Suggest that your teammate lead one song, and the rest of the team will sing along.
2. Encourage your team member to take the class and figure out how it can be incorporated into the classroom curriculum.
3. Practice getting comfortable with observation by observing one another during classroom time. Remind your teammate that she is the expert on her classroom and that parents are usually feeling self-conscious, too.
4. Encourage your team member to start small, or ask a tech-savvy colleague for a tutorial.

What would risk taking look like in your team? The following reflection will guide you through this conversation with your team. Take ten to fifteen minutes at the start of a team meeting to fill out Section A individually, then share your responses. When your team members have a sense of everyone's professional comfort level, you can begin to support one another in your growth and set concrete goals in Section B.

Reflection: Risk Taking

Section A: Complete individually

How do you define risk?

What would taking risks look like in your professional life?

What would taking risks look like in the classroom?

Section B: Complete as a team

Take turns listening to each teacher's risks, and offer ideas for a safety net for each. What could you do to allow your teammate to take professional risks?

Set one concrete goal for taking a risk in the classroom.

Fair, Respectful, and Kind

The longer you are a leader in the field of early childhood, the more teachers you will see come and go. Some years your team will feel almost effortless to manage, while other teams can feel like a constant challenge. It's likely that you will sometimes have team members who are hard to get along with.

I have learned that my team functions better when I do not expect my team members to be my friends or hope they will like me. Instead, I hope that my team members feel that I am fair, respectful, and kind. If I can be these three things every day, friendships may develop over time. But my goal is not to be liked; rather, my goal is to create a place of optimal learning for young children, teachers, and families. Shifting the focus in this way allows you the freedom to be the lead advocate for children and families, while still caring for your team as valued professionals.

Tools for the Team

Try setting up a Vulnerability Board. Place a chalkboard or dry-erase board in a private shared space, such as a coat closet or kitchen. Each team member has a different color marker to use. The board is not meant to start conversations or elicit responses, rather, it is meant to make visible the internal struggles we all face.

Here are some examples of things team members might write:

- "I'm worried that my son is doing poorly in school."
- "I'm afraid I'm not doing a good job."
- "I'm afraid others are judging me."
- "I worry at night about finances and can't sleep."

The rules of the board are as follows:

- Use "I" statements only.
- Speak for yourself only, not others.
- Do not respond on the board.
- Wipe off comments every week or so and start over.

It's a powerful thing to expose your fears. It allows team members to have more compassion for one another and build the trust necessary for open communication.

Common Language

A common language consists of the terms and phrases you use as a team to describe the work you are doing together. This shared language becomes a kind of shorthand communication, and it bonds you as professionals. A common language is important in the field of early childhood because educators have such differing experience and education. You can support children's learning outcomes by communicating easily about what and how you teach.

The list of educational terms that follows includes both terms being used in education generally and terms specific to early childhood. This list is just a start; the language you share with your team will be specific to your context and to the demographics of the children you serve. A Montessori school will have a unique set of terms each teacher needs to understand, as will a Resources for Infant Educarers (RIE), Reggio Emilia, or public pre-K program.

A lead teacher can use this list to start a conversation in a team meeting by sharing it and highlighting any terms that are especially relevant, or by sharing other terms from trainings or certifications. A lead teacher can also choose to focus on one term at a time and tie it into the work the team is doing in any given week. Simply by introducing these concepts and incorporating them into your vocabulary, you begin to have a common language.

Terms to know:

Backward design, also called *backward planning* or *backward mapping,* is a process that educators use to design **learning experiences** and instructional techniques to achieve specific learning goals. Backward design begins with the objectives of a unit or course—what students are expected to learn and be able to do—and then proceeds "backward" to create lessons that achieve those desired goals.

Brain-based learning refers to teaching methods, lesson designs, and school programs that are based on the latest scientific research about how the brain learns, including such factors as cognitive development—how students learn differently as they age, grow, and mature socially, emotionally, and cognitively.

In **child-guided learning** experiences, children make decisions about what they want to do, what they want to use or explore, and which classmates they want to play with. They make choices about their own learning, while teachers provide support. Children explore their interests, practice skills, and use previously built knowledge. Teachers can provide materials that expand on the child's interest and ask questions to further children's thinking. Teachers are involved, but children's interests direct the experience.

Community-based learning refers to a wide variety of instructional methods and programs that educators use to connect what is being taught in schools to their surrounding communities, including local institutions, history, literature, cultural heritage, and natural environments. Community-based learning is also motivated by the belief that all communities have intrinsic educational assets and resources that educators can use to enhance learning experiences for students.

A **critical friend** is typically a colleague or another educational professional, such as a **school coach**, who is committed to helping an educator or a school improve. A critical friend is someone who is encouraging and supportive, but who also provides honest and often candid feedback that may be uncomfortable or difficult to hear. In short, a critical friend is someone who agrees to speak truthfully but constructively about weaknesses, problems, and emotionally charged issues.

Developmentally appropriate practice (DAP) is the use of teaching strategies that are based on knowledge of how young children develop and learn, what makes each child unique, and the child's community and family culture and home language.

Differentiation refers to a wide variety of teaching techniques and lesson adaptations that educators use to instruct a diverse group of students with diverse learning needs in the same course, classroom, or **learning environment**.

Expanded learning time, also called *extended learning time,* refers to any educational program or strategy intended to increase the amount of time students are learning, especially for the purposes of improving academic achievement and test scores, or reducing **learning loss**, **learning gaps**, and **achievement gaps**.

In education, the term **high expectations**, or the phrase *common high expectations*, typically refers to any effort to set the same high educational standards for all students in a class, a school, or an **education system**. The concept of high expectations is premised on the philosophical and pedagogical belief that a failure to hold all students to high expectations effectively denies them **access** to a high-quality education, since the educational achievement of students tends to rise or fall in direct relation to the expectations placed on them.

Professional Dialogue

Professional dialogue is the conversation you have as a team discussing the curriculum, individual children's needs, classroom management, and what is happening in the field outside your classroom. This is the time you spend building up your common language and connecting to the big picture of the field of early childhood education.

It's valuable and informative to explore what others in our profession are doing, especially when they're doing things differently than we are. Public preschools, Montessori, Waldorf, RIE, Reggio Emilia—all these philosophies have something to teach us and can help us enrich the experiences of the young children whose learning is entrusted to us every day. Exploring advances in child development, neuroscience, and kinetic learning enlivens our knowledge and gives us new tools to use in our classrooms. When teams engage in this type of conversation, they allow inspiration to occur.

This type of dialogue requires a commitment to regular meetings as a team. If you don't have team meeting time built into your schedule, it's worth making the time to meet weekly. It's impossible to have these conversations while supervising children. Scheduling even one hour a week to have professional conversations before or after school is an investment that will yield rich dividends.

Peaceful Conflict

Peaceful conflict is the ability to accept, and even welcome, conflict in your team as a means to build trust, develop compassion, and learn from mistakes. This is a skill that you can develop in yourself and in your team. Conflict is something you will encounter in any team. Lead teachers bear the responsibility to mediate conflicts fairly and to model compassion. The reflection questions on interests versus positions (page 46) and the listening exercise (page 40) will help you approach conflict in a constructive way.

The following reflection will help you define your approach to conflict and determine how you can improve your peaceful conflict mediation skills. This is a good exercise to do alone and then with your team. Discovering how each of your team members responds to conflict will help you resolve conflict peacefully.

Reflection: Peaceful Conflict

How do you define conflict?

What did conflict look like in your household when you were growing up?

What does conflict look like in your home now?

How comfortable are you with conflict on a scale of 1 to 10, with 1 being extremely uncomfortable and 10 being completely at ease?

What are your first reactions to conflict between children? Between adults?

What do you need in order to resolve conflict?

Do you need resolution to move on after conflict?

Think of the personal relationship in your life that has the most conflict. Name three things about this person that make your relationship a challenge.

Does your own personality include any of these qualities?

If someone in your life is upset, do you often assume the cause was something you said or did? Why?

How do you want to approach conflict in our team?

From *Team Teaching in Early Childhood: Leadership Tools for Reflective Practice* by Uniit Carruyo, © 2017.

Published by Redleaf Press, www.redleafpress.org. This page may be reproduced for classroom use only.

Conversations about conflict take courage, but the benefits they yield are worth the effort. All the conversations you have in your team build trust, brick by brick. The payoff is a smoothly functioning team committed to personal growth that provides the optimum setting for young children's learning and supportive relationships with families.

Professional Development

The final element necessary for a healthy, effective team is participating in professional development, which is any formal or informal learning with professional growth as its goal. Classroom management, child development, health and safety, continued degrees or certifications, and professional learning communities are all examples of professional development.

Early childhood as a field is moving in the direction of increased education standards for teachers. Many programs and licenses require a certain amount of continuing education credits to maintain good standing with accreditors. Yet for many early childhood educators, the cost of this learning is prohibitive, and funding is scarce. We can be creative about our professional development, and with some planning, we can use the resources right in our own communities. In this section, you will find some ideas to create opportunities for learning with the resources already in place in your program.

Professional Learning Communities (PLCs)

PLC is a form of professional development in which a group of colleagues support one another's development as teachers by meeting regularly to observe one another, offer feedback, and discuss methods of improving outcomes for children and families. Your team can be its own PLC by using the tools provided in this book, doing reflections together, and making it a priority to dig deep in your team meetings. To enrich the conversation, you can branch out to include others in your program. For example, if you are feeling inspired to start a PLC, you could post a note or send an e-mail like the following to your colleagues:

What: toddler professional learning community (PLC)

Who: any toddler teacher

When: next Tuesday, 4:30 to 5:30 p.m.

Where: staff lounge

Why: to discuss ways to improve instruction and student outcomes in our classrooms

Next week's topic: gross-motor movement in the classroom

How: sharing ideas, resources, and curiosity

Other topics might include the following:

- how to support breastfeeding mothers
- engaging the senses: using art to teach concepts to infants and toddlers
- supporting early literacy
- book making
- anything you are excited about

The Unconference

Unlike a traditional conference, an unconference (also called an edcamp) is a participant-oriented meeting in which the attendees choose the agenda, discussion topics, workshops, and often even the time and venues (Budd et al. 2015). The event should be flexible, transparent, dialogue- and interaction-based, and led by the participants.

These dynamic events make professional development accessible and driven by teachers' interests. They allow for organic discoveries to be made. A simple way to organize this is to have all the teaching staff write on a sticky note what they want to discuss, then stick all the notes on a whiteboard or wall. Divide the notes loosely into topic areas to dictate groups. Invite volunteer facilitators to start the conversation and keep it on track (Kalesse 2014).

For example, if your center or school decides to do an unconference, and you choose the topic early literacy, each classroom team or each teacher (depending on the size of the program) could bring one thing to share with the group. One classroom might share a book-making project the children did, one group might share about a program in which parents visit and read to children, and so on.

Other topics might be outdoor education, science for infants and toddlers, art, cultural celebrations, food preparation, or anything at all that is of interest to the community. The idea is to make it fun and informal. Give equal time (about twenty minutes) for each group to share and answer questions about their topic.

This type of exercise is effective for early childhood educators because it provides an informal forum for teachers to learn from one another and practice public speaking. It also allows teachers to practice facilitating conversation and engaging staff members in collegial dialogue. Early childhood educators are often isolated, spending the majority of their professional time with children. The unconference is one solution to this isolation. The more we prioritize learning from our colleagues and sharing ideas, the more children and families can benefit from our collective experience.

Peer Observations

A peer observation is a period of time dedicated to simply observing another colleague at work in the classroom. Teams can rotate through observing and being observed and follow up at a team meeting with questions or comments.

When working with children, even the most experienced teachers can't see everything that is happening at any given moment. Young children require our full attention, and while seasoned teachers keep the entire room in view, we inevitably miss details. Teachers also develop habits over time, and a fresh perspective can help us see ourselves in a different light or cause us to examine more closely decisions we make in the classroom. The combination of observing, documenting the observation with a guide like the one on page 76, and then taking time for discussion after the observation is a form of learning for both the observer and the observed.

On the following page is an example of a peer observation guide:

Name: Instructional coach:

Date: Time of observation:

Home classroom: Peer classroom:

---

1. List the first things that catch your eye about this classroom:

    a.

    b.

    c.

2. What are the similarities to your home classroom?

3. What are the differences between the two classrooms?

4. What do you admire about what this team is doing in the classroom?

5. What do you think could be improved in this classroom?

6. Do you have any questions for the team? Include any additional comments on back of form.

Feedback

Feedback is a dynamic communication process occurring between two individuals that conveys information regarding the receiver's performance in work-related tasks (Baker et al. 2013). Feedback is used both to encourage existing performance attributes and to recommend changes.

Feedback is often seen as something to be feared—difficult to give and difficult to receive. But feedback is an essential part of team teaching, so it's useful to see feedback as a supportive tool, not a threat. If we look closely at this definition of feedback, it includes any individuals engaging in work together. So, for our purposes, feedback is information regarding the performance of both lead teachers and assistant teachers. For our teams to reach their maximum potential, feedback must be invited from and shared with all members of the team, and not given only from lead teachers to assistant teachers.

In the context of early childhood education, feedback can be any information about the manner in which a teacher is engaging with the classroom environment, children, families, or colleagues. Feedback could be as simple as discussing appropriate language to use with a certain age group, learning what is typical for a particular program or philosophy, or keeping conversations with families constructive and supportive. Feedback could be discussing the manner in which a lead is communicating with other team members or structuring classroom systems. Any information that helps educators provide the best care for children and the most connection with families is feedback.

To be effective, feedback must be part of a cyclical process and fit the following description:

- timely
- nonthreatening
- action-oriented
- multidimensional
- followed up

This figure is a visual representation of the feedback cycle. This applies to any member of the team giving feedback to any other member. The following sections will break down giving and receiving feedback from the perspective of the lead teacher and the perspective of the assistant teacher.

The Lead Teacher: Systems for Constructive Feedback

Giving and receiving feedback is a skill for every member of a team, but the responsibility for putting a feedback system in place falls to the lead teacher. Team leaders can set a collaborative tone and work to create a classroom culture in which feedback is simply an ordinary part of the conversation. Administrators are there for support, but team leaders are the first, most influential presence in a team's dynamic and performance.

The first step in establishing a feedback system is preventing problems by offering information and clarity to team members up front. In Montessori settings, we talk a lot about "preparing the environment" for children to learn and be successful, so children can build confidence and competency. Preparing the environment for adults is also important for a team to be successful.

You can lay the foundation of good communication by talking with your team before they are even in the classroom. Start by meeting with your team and discussing your philosophy of education, your goals for the children, and your vision of the thriving classroom. You can go over the basics of being in the classroom—what language to use in various situations and what the ground rules are for the children in your program—and define your roles as teachers using the preceding chapters as a guide. This work together will provide the framework for the feedback that will inevitably occur later. If you have already been working in your team for a while, that's okay. It's fine to present these ideas to your team as a way to strengthen your communication and positively shift any dynamic you already have in place.

You can use the following reflection to gather information from your team members about their goals. This information will help you begin conversations that include feedback. The lead teacher can ask that every member, including herself, fill out the reflection. Then devote a team meeting to sharing these reflections with one another.

Reflection: Goal Setting for Teachers

What are your strengths as a teacher?

What unique qualities do you bring to your classroom?

What are three goals you have for developing your teaching practice?

What do you need in order to accomplish those goals?

With what area of teaching do you struggle?

What do you need in order to grow in this area?

Is there anything specific I can do to support your professional growth in our classroom?

From *Team Teaching in Early Childhood: Leadership Tools for Reflective Practice* by Uniit Carruyo, © 2017.
Published by Redleaf Press, www.redleafpress.org. This page may be reproduced for classroom use only.

The Assistant Teacher: Engaging in Feedback

For assistant teachers, giving feedback to the lead teacher can feel intimidating. But this feedback is essential so lead teachers can grow as leaders and learn to better support assistant teachers. While the lead teacher may have more specialized training or more years of experience, no educator, regardless of job title, is ever done learning.

Feedback should be frequent, friendly, and supportive. This can be challenging if you have an emotional reaction to something that happens in the classroom. In early childhood, we bring to our work our whole hearts, as well as deeply held beliefs about what young children need in order to learn. When our hearts are so inextricably tied to the work we do, it's natural for emotions to factor into our decision making.

That's why it's necessary to reflect on your beliefs and *respond, not react*, to each situation as it comes up. The difference between reacting and responding is simply reflection. A reaction is an automatic response, done immediately and without thought. A response is an intentional action taken after reflecting on the various factors that contribute to a particular scenario. A response also takes into consideration a positive outcome for all involved. This takes practice, and it's a skill you can develop. Teams grow stronger when members begin to take care with one another. This is especially important for new teachers in their first few years of teaching who are building confidence and collaborative skills. It is also best to keep these conversations for the beginning or end of the day, while teachers are not directly supervising children.

Here are some things to keep in mind when delivering feedback to team members:

- Be calm and open.
- Depersonalize the feedback by using your shared beliefs (your school's philosophy, research, your organization's ground rules) as your guide and foundation.
- Make space for conversation and take time to listen to your team member's thoughts and ideas, rather than just giving your feedback and ending the conversation.
- Invite feedback from your colleague in return.
- Clearly state action items for yourself and your colleague.

Teams can also use feedback as opportunities to deepen learning. Offering concrete materials, such as articles or books, might help a teammate better understand your perspective. More and more trainings are available online, as well as back issues of early childhood publications. You can refer to these when discussing common issues that come up in early childhood classrooms. Action items can also accompany feedback—for example, committing to documenting observations of children, making a shift in classroom responsibilities, or scheduling a follow-up conversation. Following up a few days later is essential, to check in with one another and make sure everyone is on the same page.

It's essential to keep feedback multidimensional. That means you are not only giving feedback, but you are also inviting feedback (Baker et al. 2013). If you are open to feedback, in the course of your conversation you will probably hear ideas for adjustments you can make in order to be clearer, more supportive, or both. You can ask, "What can I do to support you with this?" or "Is there anything I can do to get you the tools you need?" or "What am I doing that's helpful to you, so I can keep doing it?" or "What am I doing that's unhelpful, so I can stop doing it?" Feedback can occur between peers, between mentors and mentees, and between teachers and administrators.

The Check-In Meeting

Another facet of regular feedback is to prioritize time for each team member to meet with the lead teacher in a one-on-one check-in meeting. The check-in meeting is an effective way to keep feedback nonthreatening—and keep it happening—by normalizing it as part of the routine. Scheduling predictable one-on-one check-in meetings with your team provides a forum for frequent feedback conversations. If you are not in the habit of exchanging feedback, and you suddenly schedule a meeting to talk, this can feel threatening and uncomfortable for both of you. But if you have biweekly or monthly one-on-one meetings, they feel more comfortable. This strategy also builds trust by making sure feedback is personalized and private. If you meet often, just twenty minutes makes a difference. If you can meet only monthly, try to make your meetings a little longer—at least thirty minutes.

The check-in meeting is the appropriate time and place to bring up specifics, such as specific strategies for the assistant teacher to experiment with, brainstorming about working with particular children, or going deeper into child development or philosophy. Most of the time, people are very happy to have a few minutes to talk about their perspective on how things are going in the classroom, and they find it validating and supportive. While these check-ins are designed for one-on-one conversation, they strengthen the team by making sure every member has time and space to reflect with the team leader. The mark of a great team is not the absence of conflict but rather the willingness to accept one another's differences and work together toward a common goal. In our case, the common goal is to facilitate the best outcomes for the children in our care.

Regular check-in meetings will accomplish the following important goals:

- support the lead teacher's role as the team's visionary
- allow all team members to practice skills such as listening, giving constructive feedback, and receiving feedback from one another
- create a space for the lead teacher to give guidance about classroom expectations and receive feedback on improving leadership skills
- create a forum for assistant teachers to give and receive feedback to leads and have personalized conversations about their teaching practice
- allow compassion to develop by prioritizing listening to others' perspectives
- provide a running document of the team's professional growth by keeping track of any individual goals team members set
- allow trust to build between team members, which increases job satisfaction and productivity
- allow team members to feel valued and heard by dedicating one-on-one time
- allow space for questions and reflection about what is going on in the classroom
- create a safe, private space for team members to share any personal information that may be affecting their experience

Giving and receiving feedback is a valuable skill in education, especially when we are working closely in teams. The following feedback protocol can help your team conceptualize the check-in meeting or introduce the idea to your program.

Feedback Protocol for Team Check-Ins

The eight steps for a check-in meeting are as follows:

1. Find a confidential space to talk one-on-one with your team member.
2. Ask, "How are things going for you in the classroom?"
3. Listen without interrupting.
4. Paraphrase what you heard so your teammate knows you listened and understood.

5. Wait for your teammate's response.
6. At this point, you may have some action items; state them clearly and commit to following through.
7. Ask, "Is there something I can do to support you more?"
8. Listen to your teammate's answer.

Here are some guidelines to keep in mind for check-in meetings:

- It's important to be respectful of the time by beginning and ending on time. If you have more to talk about, schedule a follow-up conversation.
- The check-in meeting is time set aside specifically for assistant teachers to share and reflect.
- The role of the lead teacher in check-in meetings is to listen.
- Regardless of who is speaking, practicing active listening is important for developing communication skills.

The following checklist will help you imagine what active listening looks like, and avoid common mistakes that can prevent you from truly listening:

- Sit still, with no distractions.
- Make eye contact.
- Stay present and focused.
- Watch for nonverbal signals such as nervous fidgeting and other body language.

Avoid doing these things during active listening:

- judging
- rehearsing a response
- thinking of advice to give
- thinking of something else
- talking or arguing or defending yourself
- planning how to fix the situation
- checking your phone
- interrupting
- making the conversation about you or taking things personally
- veering off on a tangent

Here's how to reflect what someone has said:

- Start by saying, "I hear you saying that..." or "It sounds like you feel...."

- Paraphrase slightly, and try to capture exactly what the speaker said without adding anything.
- Avoid interpreting or assuming you know what the speaker might be feeling; simply repeat what the speaker said so she knows you were listening and she was heard.

During a check-in meeting, your team member may come to you with concerns or complaints about other colleagues, personal stories to share, or ideas for the classroom. Most of the time, people like to have this time to talk and connect. Some team members may be more action oriented and may find it uncomfortable to sit one-on-one and talk. If you have a team member like this, you can accommodate her by doing more active working meetings. For example, you might use the time to walk through your classroom or other school space and hear your team member's ideas for improving the environment or curriculum. Or you might use the time to plan a school or family event with your action-oriented team member while chatting about how things are going.

Tools for Teams: Gratitude Buckets

Place a small basket or bucket for each team member (labeled by name) in a shared space, such as the classroom closet or a shelf in the classroom. Keep slips of paper and a pen nearby, and at least once a week, spend a few minutes writing out gratitude notes to each of your team members. This is a way to acknowledge the great things your teammates are doing and to reinforce your shared vision for the classroom. Notes might say things like the following:

- "Thank you for being calm and patient with the children during that moment of chaos!"
- "I'm grateful for your sense of humor in our classroom."
- "Thank you for always greeting families with a smile."
- "I'm grateful for your warmth with the children in our classroom."

Gratitude is especially important to practice on the hard days when everything feels like a challenge. Thanking your teammates for their contributions will build trust and help everyone feel more valued. The gratitude notes also help develop your team's identity by stating explicitly what is celebrated in your particular classroom.

Regularly talking about the things the team is doing well is an important morale booster. It's easy to fixate on what's wrong. The team will be much more receptive to tune-ups if a feeling of positivity is established in the classroom by talking regularly about what is going well.

Tools for Teams: What Went Well?

At the beginning or end of any team meeting, take a moment to go around the circle and have each team member list three things that went well that day or week in the classroom. This gives everyone an excellent window into what individuals on the team are experiencing as positive so team members can make sure to keep doing it.

This is effective in and of itself, or you could extend the activity when you are implementing something new in the program. After introducing some new system or routine, team leaders can ask individuals to list two things that went well and one thing that could be improved. This strategy creates space for constructive dialogue and feedback while keeping the tone of the conversation positive.

For example, if you introduce a sensory table to your classroom, that week's exercise might look like the following. A team member describes two things that went well with the sensory table and one thing that could be improved:

- "The child who was having some behavior issues in the classroom was busy and engaged at the sensory table all week."
- "The sensory table gives us a new option for redirection in our classroom."
- "One thing that could be improved is keeping a small hand broom and dishpan hanging next to the table so children can learn to clean up when they spill the table's contents."

Using Surveys to Generate Feedback

Surveys are a simple tool for gathering feedback as a team. They can be an effective way to inform changes in your classroom or program. A scheduled midpoint check-in is useful not only to normalize feedback in the team's routine but also to catch anything that might be veering off course. With a brief midpoint survey, you can get a sense of what is working and make adjustments immediately, rather than waiting until the end of the year to survey your team or families.

The midpoint survey is intended for the lead teacher to get feedback from the assistant teachers. For example, the lead can solicit feedback in December from assistant teachers before winter break. She can then make any necessary adjustments or address concerns before or at the start of the new year. If assistant teachers have concerns that require more than minor adjustments, the lead teacher can schedule a longer check-in to address these concerns and start the second half of the year with growth as a priority.

Midpoint Team Check-In Survey

On a scale of 1 to 5, with 1 being poor, 2 to 4 being good, and 5 being excellent, rate the following aspects of our classroom. Please include any specifics in the space provided.

Prepared learning environment for children: 1   2   3   4   5

Clarity of roles within our team: 1   2   3   4   5

Cooperation and collaboration in our team: 1   2   3   4   5

Support for your professional growth by lead teacher: 1   2   3   4   5

Trusting bonds with families, relationships with families nurtured: 1   2   3   4   5

Alignment of our classroom with philosophy, best practices, and current research: 1   2   3   4   5

Space made for each team member to make meaningful contributions to the classroom: 1   2   3   4   5

Anything else you'd like me to know: 1   2   3   4   5

You can also use a survey at the end of the year to gather information for planning the next school year. Several free, easy online survey builders are available. You can either e-mail these or give hard copies to your team. Survey-Monkey is one free resource that can also help organize the data afterward. Microsoft Word includes templates to create your own surveys that can be used online or printed and handed to families, depending on preference and accessibility. Inviting people's opinions of the work you do can be scary. Through surveys, your team can gain a lot of insight into your professional impact and impress people with your fearless approach to learning. Your use of surveys is also an invitation to others in your program to incorporate feedback into their learning style.

Team Year-End Feedback Survey

Your name:

Your title:

Please list three things you love about working in this classroom.

Please list three things that could be improved in this classroom.

Do you feel supported in your role in this classroom? If yes, in what ways?

Is there anything I can do to be more supportive of your role in this classroom?

What advice would you give to a teacher starting out in your position in this classroom?

From *Team Teaching in Early Childhood: Leadership Tools for Reflective Practice* by Uniit Carruyo, © 2017.
Published by Redleaf Press, www.redleafpress.org. This page may be reproduced for classroom use only.

Do you feel children get what they need in this classroom? Give examples.

Do you feel families get what they need from this classroom? Give examples.

Do you think we function as a team in this classroom? Give examples.

Is there anything else you'd like me to know?

Thank you for taking the time to share your thoughts with me! I appreciate learning from you and working to improve our classroom.

From *Team Teaching in Early Childhood: Leadership Tools for Reflective Practice* by Uniit Carruyo, © 2017.
Published by Redleaf Press, www.redleafpress.org. This page may be reproduced for classroom use only.

The following survey is intended for classroom teams to use with families. When your team has the results back, use a team meeting to go through the feedback and see if there are any adjustments you could make to your environment or communication style to improve families' and children's experiences. For example, you might learn that your families prefer to get a phone call about their child, rather than an e-mail, and you might decide to give future families the option of receiving information via phone or e-mail.

Year-End Family Survey

Your name:

Were you satisfied with your child's experience in this classroom?

Do you feel that your child grew emotionally, academically, and physically in this classroom?

Please list three things you liked about your experience with this classroom.

Please list three things that could be improved in this classroom.

Do you feel that we were supportive of your child and family this year? Give examples.

From *Team Teaching in Early Childhood: Leadership Tools for Reflective Practice* by Uniit Carruyo, © 2017.
Published by Redleaf Press, www.redleafpress.org. This page may be reproduced for classroom use only.

Is there anything I can do to be more supportive of you and your family?

What advice would you give a new family starting out in this classroom?

What do you think made the biggest impact on your child's learning in our classroom?

Is there anything else you'd like me to know?

Thank you for taking the time to share your thoughts with me. I appreciate your perspective and am committed to continuously improving children's learning in my classroom.

From *Team Teaching in Early Childhood: Leadership Tools for Reflective Practice* by Uniit Carruyo, © 2017.

Published by Redleaf Press, www.redleafpress.org. This page may be reproduced for classroom use only.

Surveys conducted at the beginning of implementing something new provide a baseline of expectations. Surveys done in the middle of a process keep things on track and in line with the mission and vision, and allow for any necessary course correcting. Surveys conducted at the end of a process help the team reflect on what was accomplished and plan for future iterations. Surveys are a free, straightforward way to gain insight about the professional work your team is doing.

Team Meetings

In early childhood, time together as professionals is often hard to come by, as we are usually directly supervising children's learning. Any early childhood teacher knows that finishing a sentence—let alone an entire conversation—when speaking to a colleague during the school day can often be impossible. Depending on the age you work with and the schedule of your program, there may be a particular time of day that is more conducive to conversation. It might be naptime or when the children leave the classroom for special activities.

More likely, your team meetings will happen before or after the school day. In my experience, team meetings are simultaneously the hardest and the most important things to schedule. This dilemma calls for creativity and commitment from all involved. It's important to be extremely efficient with your meeting time and to be as intentional as possible with your agenda. Your teammates are more likely to make the time to meet regularly if they feel their time is well spent and meetings are satisfying rather than draining.

In chapter 5, we talked about strategies for one-on-one meeting time with team members. Here, let's take a look at some strategies for meeting with your entire team.

The Facilitator's Role

The lead teacher acts as facilitator and sets the agenda. The agenda will include anything relevant to the team. That could mean discussing one child or family whose needs are not being met in the classroom, dividing or redistributing responsibilities, or solving conundrums that arise in day-to-day work with young children. The agenda could also include professional development or sharing of resources. Most people appreciate having an idea of the agenda ahead of time, even something as simple and informal as bullet points on a whiteboard or a note posted in a private shared space.

The facilitator also sets the tone of the conversation, keeps the conversation on track, and strives to maintain balance in the group by making sure no one is dominating the conversation or staying silent. Team leaders should share along with everyone else but should never be the dominant speaker. If the meeting is balanced, everyone shares more or less equally. Some people are more talkative, and some people are shier, but in small groups, most people feel safe enough to share comfortably. If you notice people need a little more time to share, you can extend a topic a little. If you notice that people are veering off topic, you can direct the conversation back to the agenda. There will be a learning curve as you get to know your team and everyone's comfort level increases.

The facilitator is also responsible for starting and ending the meeting on time. This is a gesture of respect for the participants' valuable time.

There will be times when a topic or question comes up that causes the group to fall silent. Silence may feel intimidating to you as a facilitator, because keeping the meeting on track is your responsibility. With practice, you will begin to see that good things come out of silence. Rather than rushing to fill the silence or move to the next topic, practice waiting and seeing what happens. Often someone will chime in after five, ten, or fifteen seconds and set off another wave of interesting comments. As a challenge to yourself when facilitating, see how long you can wait comfortably for the conversation to continue.

"Park" any off-topic items on a "parking lot" list to address at a later time. This strategy allows your team to keep conversation flowing forward and avoid veering off on tangents. It's easy to get sidetracked, and when that happens, the meeting is no longer effective and focused. If someone starts heading off track, or if multiple other issues are coming up, you can simply say, "This feels like an important topic we should devote more time to. Let's put it on the agenda for the next meeting. Do you want to add anything about it before we move on?"

That said, sometimes an unexpected topic comes up and needs to be addressed right away. As the facilitator, you can make the call to either divert the group or park the topic.

At the end of the meeting, summarize the discussion to bring closure to the conversation. Acknowledge your own action items and the action items of others. Establish a time to follow up on any items in the parking lot. This follow-up can be as simple as an e-mail, or it might be the next scheduled meeting.

This section gives you the basic structure for facilitating a meeting. If a meeting is a machine, the protocols described in the following sections are the grease that gets and keeps the gears rolling. Protocols are ways to add personality and interest to meetings. You can use protocols at the beginning of a meeting or throughout it, depending on the agenda.

Protocols are useful tools when you are trying to encourage conversation in a group of people. These work for both small and large groups, but here we will focus on using them in a team of two to five teachers. These protocols can serve as icebreakers when you are developing trust in your team. Over time they can evolve into familiar routines that create a safe space where everyone on the team feels heard.

Clearing Protocol

Clearings are a simple way to keep the communication flowing and build trust among your team. The clearing protocol is an exercise in which the participants take turns briefly summing up what they bring with them, figuratively, into that particular meeting on that particular day (McDonald et al. 2007). Sometimes, depending on the day and the amount of trust in the group, team members may share quite personal thoughts. If someone shares feelings of exhaustion after being up all night with an infant at home, or someone shares the news of a spouse's job loss, or someone is just having a bad day, the meeting starts with an attitude of support. The simple act of giving someone attention for a moment is a useful way to set the tone of the meeting with compassion.

An important aspect of this exercise is that participants are not invited to respond to what other participants share. The expectation is that the group will give each member quiet attention and practice active listening and then move to the next member without comment. This clearing exercise serves multiple purposes:

- It keeps the meeting moving on track without detours into personal conversations.
- It allows people to share without having to answer questions or follow up if they don't feel comfortable doing so.
- It allows people to get any rants off their chests before the meeting starts, without engaging in debate on hot-button issues.
- It allows participants a moment to share personal information in an otherwise professionally focused meeting.
- It affords members of the group an opportunity to feel heard.
- It builds trust.
- It provides a transition from teaching mode to listening and sharing mode.
- It allows group members to see things from other members' perspectives; hearing what members prioritize to share gives a candid look at what members value.
- It balances the power dynamic by letting each member contribute something meaningful.

- It encourages contributions from people who would otherwise remain quiet during a meeting, and it builds confidence in members who find it difficult to speak in front of a group.
- It creates a space for compassion to grow in the team through hearing what members are experiencing from their own perspective.

Members always have the option to pass on sharing anything. They can share as much or as little as they choose, as long as they keep the length of each clearing to a couple of minutes. Although people have the option to pass, most people love the opportunity to share in this type of setting, and it's amazing to hear from people who are typically very shy in meetings.

The exercise may take the first ten to fifteen minutes of a meeting, but it is a worthwhile investment of time. If you have a tight agenda and don't want to sacrifice the clearing, you could also set a timer to keep things on track.

A variation on this protocol, once your team is familiar with the process, is to ask people to choose just one word that sums up how they feel that day. Let that be the introduction to the meeting. The one-word clearing protocol works best when the tone is light and there is nothing serious to address.

Pair-Share Protocol

The pair-share protocol works well when team members are just getting to know one another. This protocol is simply pairing up and sharing on a topic in quick, timed increments. For example, your team might have two pairs. Tell your team each pair will have three minutes to share one thing. Then you can share with the larger group interesting things that came up. Have participants share their partners' contributions rather than their own. This works well for people who are shy. One-on-one conversation is often much less threatening than group conversation, and it's often easier to speak for someone else than for oneself.

Here are some ideas for pair-share topics when your team is first building trust:

- What is one memory you have about your own early childhood education?
- What is your favorite thing about being a teacher?
- Where do you fall in your family's birth order, and how does that inform your teaching style?
- What do you see yourself doing professionally in three years?

Once your team has built some trust, topics can dig deeper, as in the following examples:

- What did discipline look like in your household when you were growing up?
- What is the hardest thing for you about working with young children?
- What do you wish to improve about your teaching practice?
- What would you do if you could not teach?

Speak-Listen-Observe Protocol

This is a protocol to help team members practice active listening. You need one or more groups of three for this protocol. In each trio, the members take turns being the speaker, the listener, and the observer. Each team member plays each role once. You introduce a topic, such as, "Tell a story of a time when you felt sad." The speaker tells the story, the listener listens, and the observer watches both and notes tone of voice, body language, facial expression, and language of both the speaker and the listener. After everyone has had a turn at each role, the participants take turns sharing what they noticed when they were the observer.

This is a great way to get a sense of your teammates' backgrounds, personalities, and listening styles. Sometimes different people will give different accounts of the same story. This protocol brings attention to how easy it is to mishear someone.

You can play with this protocol and try it different ways. For example, have the listeners refrain from responding or reacting in one round, and in another round encourage them to make eye contact, nod, lean forward, mirror body language, and make listening sounds ("Mm-hmm," "Huh," "Ah," and so on). Then you can have the speakers share whether they felt more or less heard depending on the response of the listener. You can keep the tone light or serious based on the questions you ask the group to share. This is an important protocol to time because it's easy to lose track of time once the conversation gets rolling.

Here are some ideas for topics:

- Tell me about a time when you felt empowered.
- Tell me about a time when you felt afraid.
- Tell me about a time when you had to make a tough decision.
- Tell me about something you did that you are proud of.

- Tell me about someone who has been a powerful influence on you.
- Tell me about a defining moment in your career.
- Tell me about something you love.

This exercise helps teachers learn and practice good listening skills. It also serves as a powerful trust builder because it invites people to share personal stories.

Self-Portrait Gallery Walk

This disarming exercise builds trust and helps your team members tap into their playful and creative sides. Have members bring paper and drawing utensils to your meeting. Ask your team to spend five minutes drawing a self-portrait, and then have them tape their portraits to a large whiteboard or wall. Give each team member a pad of sticky notes, and take five to ten minutes to view the portraits silently, as though you were at an art gallery. Use your sticky notes to write down any thoughts that come to mind when you are looking at the other self-portraits. Stick your notes on the wall near the portraits. Then walk through the gallery to read the comments people left. Take turns sharing any comments that stood out or left an impression. Have the artists talk more about their self-portraits.

Conclusion

Teamwork is a journey, not a destination. Participating effectively in a team is a skill that takes time to master. The practical teamwork skills, like holding productive meetings and running an efficient classroom, get easier with practice. Meanwhile, the truly hard work of personal growth happens in each individual's heart and mind through reflection. And individuals move at their own pace, with their own challenges to overcome.

All of us, whether we are lead teachers or assistant teachers, have the capacity to become compassionate educators who bring out the best in others—children, families, and team members. To do this, we each have to be willing to look at our own reflection, even if we sometimes don't like what we see—*especially* when we don't like what we see. When we reflect on our own motives and expectations, we see the difference between operating from our hearts and operating from our egos or from habit. We notice how much more positively influential we can be when we operate from the heart. We will continue to make many mistakes, and we can learn from every one of them when we engage in the hard work of honest reflection. This practice of reflection makes the difference between an average team that gets the job done and a team that is transformative for its members.

Maria Montessori described an intense, threefold process of preparation an adult must do in order to be the most effective teacher for children. It is a physical, intellectual, and spiritual process. She said, "We have to watch ourselves most carefully. The real preparation for education is a study of one's self. The training of the teacher who is to help life is something far more than a learning of ideas. It includes the training of character; it is a preparation of the spirit" (Montessori 1969, 132).

I believe the same is true for preparing early childhood teachers to lead and collaborate with other adults. We must investigate our own habits, our defenses, our biases, our fears, our challenges, and our deeply held beliefs to be positive guides for other teachers.

The journey is humbling, and it takes courage. I wish you courage on your journey. I hope this book will give you a mirror to help you and your team look more closely at yourselves and examine the important work you do together. I hope you will find as much joy and satisfaction in supporting the developing adults on your team as you do in developing the young children in your classrooms.

References

Association Montessori Internationale (AMI). 2016. "Montessori Quotes: Vision." http://ami-global.org/montessori/quotes/vision.

Baker, Amanda, Dominique Perreault, Alain Reid, and Céline M. Blanchard. 2013. "Feedback and Organizations: Feedback Is Good, Feedback-Friendly Culture Is Better." *Canadian Psychology* 54 (4): 260–68.

Brazeau, Gayle A. 2005. "Risk Taking: A Distinguishing Factor of *Good* versus *Great* Teachers." *American Journal of Pharmaceutical Education* 69 (4): 541–42.

Budd, Aidan, Holger Dinkel, Manuel Corpas, Jonathan C. Fuller, Laura Rubinat, Damien P. Devos, Pierre, H. Khouiery, Konrad U. Förstner, Fotis Georgatos, Francis Rowland, Malvika Sharan, Janos X. Binder, Tom Grace, Karyn Traphagen, Adam Gristwood, and Natasha T. Wood. 2015. "Ten Simple Rules for Organizing an Unconference." *PLoS Computational Biology* 11 (1): e1003905. http://journals.plos.org/ploscompbiol/article?id=10.1371/journal.pcbi.1003905.

Dewey, John. 1938. *Experience and Education*. New York: Macmillan.

DuFour, Richard, and Robert E. Eaker. 1999. *Professional Learning Communities at Work: Best Practices for Enhancing Student Achievement*. Bloomington, IN: National Educational Service.

Duignan, Brian. 2015. "Occam's Razor." In *Encyclopaedia Britannica*. http://www.britannica.com/topic/Occams-razor.

Fisher, Roger, William Ury, and Bruce Patton. 1991. *Getting to Yes: Negotiating Agreement without Giving In*. New York: Penguin Books.

Glanz, Jeffrey. 2002. *Finding Your Leadership Style: A Guide for Educators*. Alexandria, VA: USA Association for Supervision and Curriculum Development (ASCD).

Heifetz, Ronald A., and Marty Linsky. 2002. *Leadership on the Line: Staying Alive through the Dangers of Leading*. Boston, MA: Harvard Business School Press.

Ithaca Montessori School. 2016. "Mission and Philosophy." Accessed June 2. http://ithacamontessori.org/our-school/mission-philosophy/.

Jossey-Bass Inc. 2000. *The Jossey-Bass Reader on Educational Leadership*. San Francisco: Jossey-Bass.

Kalesse, Rob. 2014. "Teachers Lead the Way at Edcamps: Participant-Driven 'Unconferences' Restore the Power of Professional Development." *Reading Today* 31 (5): 20–21.

Kassner, Laura. 2014. "Opportunities to Personalize Teacher Learning: Innovative Approaches to Bridge Evaluation and Professional Development for Continuous Improvement." Metropolitan Educational Research Consortium. http://files.eric.ed.gov/fulltext/ED552977.pdf.

Maslow, Abraham H. 1943. "A Theory of Human Motivation." Research History. http://www.researchhistory.org/category/psychology.

McDonald, Joseph P., Nancy Mohr, Alan Dichter, and Elizabeth C. McDonald. 2007. *The Power of Protocols: An Educator's Guide to Better Practice.* 2nd edition. New York: Teacher's College Press.

Merriam-Webster.com. 2016. "Culture." Accessed June 3. http://www.merriam-webster.com/dictionary/culture.

Montessori, Maria. 1969. *The Absorbent Mind.* Translated from the Italian by Claude A. Claremont. New York: Dell Publishing.

———. 1972. *Education and Peace.* Chicago: Regenery.

Morris, Rick. 2014. "Sign Language Posters." http://www.newmanagement.com/main/sign_language.html.

National Head Start Association (NHSA). 2016. "About Us: Mission, Vision, History." http://www.nhsa.org/about-us/mission-vision-history.

Nhat Hanh, Thich. 1996. *Being Peace.* Berkeley CA: Parallax Press.

Rath, Tom, and Donald O. Clifton. 2004. *How Full Is Your Bucket? Positive Strategies for Work and Life.* New York: Gallup Press.

Riley, Dave, Robert R. San Juan, Joan Klinkner, and Ann Ramminger. 2008. *Social and Emotional Development: Connecting Science and Practice in Early Childhood Settings.* Saint Paul, MN: Redleaf Press.

Ruiz, Don Miguel. 1997. *The Four Agreements: A Practical Guide to Personal Freedom.* San Rafael, CA: Amber-Allen Publishing.

Sather, Susan E. 2009. *Leading Professional Learning Teams: A Start-up Guide for Improving Instruction.* Thousand Oaks, CA: Corwin Press.

Senge, Peter M. 1990. *The Fifth Discipline: The Art and Practice of the Learning Organization.* New York: Doubleday/Currency.

Seligman, Martin E. P. 2011. *Flourish: A Visionary New Understanding of Happiness and Well-Being.* New York: Free Press.

Sullivan, Susan, and Jeffrey Glanz. 2005. *Supervision That Improves Teaching: Strategies and Techniques.* Thousand Oaks, CA: Corwin Press.

Supovitz, Jonathan, and Jolley Bruce Christman. 2003. *Developing Communities of Instructional Practice: Lessons from Cincinnati and Philadelphia.* Consortium for Policy Research in Education: CPRE Policy Briefs, RB-39.

Whitaker, Todd. 2002. *Dealing with Difficult Teachers*. 2nd ed. Larchmont, NY: Eye on Education.

Wiener, Ross, and Kasia Lundy. 2014. "Survey Says: Using Teacher Feedback to Bolster Evaluation." *American Educator* 38 (1): 14–17. http://files.eric.ed .gov/fulltext/EJ1023872.pdf.

Further Reading

Boule, Michelle. 2011. *Mob Rule Learning: Camps, Unconferences, and Trashing the Talking Head*. Medford, NJ: CyberAge Books.

Brach, Tara. 2003. *Radical Acceptance: Embracing Your Life with the Heart of a Buddha*. New York: Bantam Books.

———. 2012. *True Refuge: Finding Peace and Freedom in Your Own Awakened Heart*. New York: Bantam Books.

Brown, Brené. 2013. *The Power of Vulnerability: Teachings on Authenticity, Connection, and Courage*. Louisville, CO: Sounds True Publishing.

Bstan-dzin-rgya-mtsho, Dalai Lama XIV, and Howard C. Cutler. 1998. *The Art of Happiness: A Handbook for Living*. New York: Riverhead Books.

Dalai Lama and Howard Cutler. 2003. *The Art of Happiness: A Handbook for Living*. Sydney: Hachette Australia.

Dewey, John. 1997. *Experience and Education*. New York: Free Press.

Montessori, Maria. 1969. *The Absorbent Mind*. Translated from the Italian by Claude A. Claremont. New York: Dell Publishing.

Rath, Tom, and Donald O. Clifton. 2004. *How Full Is Your Bucket? Positive Strategies for Work and Life*. New York: Gallup Press.

Ruiz, Don Miguel. 1997. *The Four Agreements: A Practical Guide to Personal Freedom*. San Rafael, CA: Amber-Allen Publishing.

Seligman, Martin E. P. 2011. *Flourish: A Visionary New Understanding of Happiness and Well-Being*. New York: Free Press.

Senge, Peter M. 2006. *The Fifth Discipline: The Art and Practice of the Learning Organization*. New York: Doubleday.

Tolle, Eckhart. 2016. *A New Earth: Awakening to Your Life's Purpose*. New York: Penguin Books.

Index